The Gaijin
Cookbook

The Gaijin Cookbook

JAPANESE RECIPES
FROM A CHEF, FATHER, EATER,
AND LIFELONG OUTSIDER

Ivan Orkin AND **Chris Ying**

Photographs by Aubrie Pick

HOUGHTON MIFFLIN HARCOURT

BOSTON ◆ NEW YORK 2019

For information about permission to reproduce selections from this book, write
to trade.permissions@hmhco.com or to Permissions, Houghton Mifflin Harcourt
Publishing Company, 3 Park Avenue, 19th Floor, New York, New York 10016.

hmhbooks.com

Library of Congress Cataloging-in-Publication Data
Names: Orkin, Ivan, author. | Ying, Chris, author. | Pick, Aubrie, photographer.
Title: The gaijin cookbook : Japanese recipes from a chef, father, eater, and lifelong
outsider / Ivan Orkin and Chris Ying ; photographs by Aubrie Pick.
Description: Boston : A Rux Martin Book, Houghton Mifflin Harcourt, [2019] |
Includes index.
Identifiers: LCCN 2019002730 (print) | LCCN 2019004086 (ebook) | ISBN
9781328954404 (ebook) | ISBN 9781328954350 (paper over board)
Subjects: LCSH: Cooking, Japanese. | LCGFT: Cookbooks.
Classification: LCC TX724.5.J3 (ebook) | LCC TX724.5.J3 07247 2019 (print) |
DDC 641.5952—dc23
LC record available at https://lccn.loc.gov/2019002730

Book design by Walter Green

Printed in China

C&C 10 9 8 7 6 5 4 3 2 1

This book is dedicated to the idea
that we will all eat much better
if we listen carefully, study broadly,
cook bravely, and share respectfully.

Contents

Introductions

Gaijin is the Japanese term for people like me.

I used to cringe when I heard it. It took years to overcome the shame of it. But these days I don't mind it so much. Partly because it doesn't really apply to me anymore. Mostly because I've come to accept it.

Gaijin (guy-jin) means "foreigner" or "outsider," but it really implies something more like "intruder." Put more stereotypically, a gaijin is a white guy, clumsily bumbling through Japan, leaving a wake of social miscues and broken dishes behind him. It's a term that's meant to be derogatory—sometimes playfully, other times with menace. And even though I've lived in Japan for the better part of three decades, speak Japanese fluently, have opened two successful ramen shops in Tokyo, and am raising three half-Japanese kids, I'm still a gaijin. I can't help it, just like I can't help being head over heels in love with Japan.

I'm not a fetishist—or maybe I am, I don't know. I've felt drawn toward Japan since I was a clueless teenage dishwasher at a Japanese restaurant in the town where I grew up on Long Island. I studied Japanese literature and language in college and moved to Tokyo almost immediately after graduation. I met my first wife while I was living in Japan. When she died, our son, Isaac, and I found comfort in returning to Japan as often as we could. Years later, on one of our trips, Isaac and I met a beautiful, brilliant designer named Mari and her son, Alex. Mari and I fell in love, got married, had our son Ren, and lived with our boys in Tokyo. In the mid-2000s, I tied my career—and the fate of my family—to Japan, opening a couple of ramen shops that somehow defied the odds and became runaway successes. The fact that a gaijin could make a killer bowl of ramen seemed to disarm and delight my customers.

In short, I've spent most of my adulthood in Japan, and it continues to exert the same irresistible force on me. We live in New York now, where I own two busy ramen restaurants, and my family has a pleasant suburban American life, but we still think about Japan constantly.

We daydream about Tokyo, where my kids had a vibrant, independent existence that helped them come into their own as people. These days I worry about maintaining a connection to their Japanese heritage, even though Mari and I have done our best to give them a bicultural upbringing. We miss our friends, who are the absolute best at having a good time and endlessly generous and compassionate whenever we need help figuring our lives out. Although my family loves the States, we look forward to our visits to Japan. We count the days until we're riding the train around Tokyo, passing whole afternoons in fancy department stores, wandering around festivals in the summer, speaking Japanese all day, visiting friends and old haunts. I sold my ramen shops in Japan, but it still makes me smile to think about my old customers and the neighborhood shopkeepers with whom I would shoot the shit in the mornings and evenings.

But, most of all, I miss the hell out of the food in Japan.

Like most professional chefs, I consider Japanese food to be the pinnacle of cuisine. It's what we want to eat all the time. We make pilgrimages to Japan to witness traditional Japanese cuisine and simultaneously marvel at the way Japanese cooks absorb and incorporate foreign influence. The Japanese own sushi, ramen, soba, udon, tempura, yakitori, kaiseki, kappo, and izakaya, but they also bake amazing pastries and produce some of the world's finest French and Italian dining. At restaurants and bars, you're as likely to drink a striking, hard-to-find natural wine as an ultrarefined sake. The high end of dining in Japan is as evolved and thrilling as anywhere on earth, while the stuff you can buy at convenience stores, food courts, and mom-and-pop shops is probably the best on the planet.

Japan also has the most active food-related publishing industry I've ever seen. Bookstore shelves—there are still big, beautiful bookstores in Japan!—are jammed with thousands of titles, from the oversize coffee-table chefs' cookbooks you get in America to specialty titles to cookbooks for kids to glossy magazines with pictures of nothing but spaghetti. I love meandering through one of Tokyo's palatial bookstores, piling up books until I can't carry any more. These same kinds of exhaustive resources about Japanese food didn't exist in English when I first moved to the country, clueless and hungry. The situation is a little better now. Shizuo Tsuji's *Japanese Cooking: A Simple Art* is my guiding star. I really like Nancy Singleton Hachisu's books, and I've always thought that Harris Salat does an admirable job of trying to translate the Japanese canon to an American audience. Oh, and *Donabe*, a recent book entirely about cooking in earthenware pots, is an incredible single-subject exploration, and I hope Naoko Takei Moore keeps sharing her knowledge with us.

But, in general, I find that Japanese food often gets treated with over-the-top reverence in English-language books, especially by my fellow gaijin, and I think that actually does the cuisine a disservice. Japanese food is not all precious, high-flying stuff. A Japanese life encompasses the same range of situations as an American one. There are busy weeknights and weekends when you feel ambitious, picky kids, special occasions, dreary winters, sweltering summers, picnics, potlucks, parties, and hangovers. And there's food for every occasion.

What I'm trying to say is that this book is not a manual for making perfect sushi or a memoir of a great summer in Kyoto. It's a reflection of a lifetime spent as an outsider looking admiringly at Japan, trying my damnedest to soak up everything I can in order to improve myself as a chef, a husband, a father, a friend—hell, as a person. I'm sharing it with you in this book because I know beyond a shadow of a doubt that my life is better for what I've learned from Japan. Even if you've never given the place much thought, so long as you're open-minded, I think I can prove that to you.

The recipes in this book are mostly drawn from what I cook at home, along with a couple favorites from my restaurants. It's not a comprehensive guide to Japanese food, but rather a story of my specific experience of it. Thus, the book is organized a little differently from other cookbooks. It's structured around the facets of Japanese life that I've come to identify with most strongly. (Don't worry, we've also included a helpful recipe list that's organized more traditionally, for those who want a different point of entry.) Here are the themes we've divided the book into:

Eat More Japanese: What does it mean to eat Japanese? To me it's not about specific foods or techniques, but rather an overarching approach to cooking. In fact, there are very few ingredients in this book that you can't find easily. (See Ingredients, page 239, for more about the pantry items you'll need.) In my experience, "cooking more Japanese" comes down to paying closer attention to details, embracing variety and seasonality, and understanding umami—the flavor usually described as the essence of savoriness. This section includes the foundational recipes and flavors that taught me to understand Japanese food—simple things like rice and dashi, and a lot of classic dishes that you're probably familiar with—plus ways that Japanese cooking can help you feed your kids in more interesting ways.

Open to Anything: There's a pervasive impression about Japanese culture that it's guarded, bordering on impenetrable. Granted, there were several centuries in Japanese history when the country officially closed itself off from the rest of the world, but I think that reputation is misguided, or at least overstated. The reason I was able to make a name for myself as a ramen chef is that Japanese cuisine can actually be incredibly receptive to foreign inspiration. There's a whole genre of Japanese "Western food" (*yoshoku*) that is born directly from outside influence, yet you and I might have trouble seeing the lines. Curry and tonkatsu (fried pork cutlets) are yoshoku, for instance. They were ideas that came to Japan, merged with local tastes and products, and emerged as something new. In America we like to call this phenomenon *fusion*, but that word implies something that's forced, which is simply not my impression of Japanese food at all. This section of the book focuses on recipes that have mingled and coalesced over time, like tipsy strangers at a really good party, eventually leading to new and delicious collaborations.

Empathy: The last thing I want to do in this book is to make sweeping statements about anybody, but I found the vast majority of the people I met while living in Japan to be overwhelmingly courteous and thoughtful. Maybe your experience of Japan is different from mine, but I really do believe that baked into Japanese society is a shared sense of responsibility for the comfort and well-being of your fellow humans. And I think that penchant for knowing how your actions will affect someone else translates into the cuisine. In other words, comfort food in Japan is the best, from simmering hot pots that warm your soul to rib-sticking rice porridge to sweet-smoky-salty braises and stews. Here is where you're going to find the recipes I make when someone I love needs some nurturing through food.

Otaku (Geeking Out): Japan is home to skilled and meticulous artists, architects, designers, and cooks who make the finest, most clever shit on the planet. It's inspirational. It's not why I moved to Japan in the first place, but it's the reason I stayed to open my own businesses and try my hand at doing one thing—ramen—really well. There are multiple Japanese words that describe people with this sort of hyperfocused dedication to their craft, but I've settled on *otaku,* or "geek." Filed under Otaku are the more intensive recipes in the book—nothing you need to commit a lifetime to mastering, but definitely dishes you'll get better and faster at producing with practice. Think dan dan noodles that take two days to make, handmade gyoza you'll spend an hour folding, and all things fried (a cooking method that is often misunderstood and unfairly maligned).

Good Times: That fanatical enthusiasm for perfecting one's craft extends to the way Japanese people cut loose. Seriously, I find that when it comes to eating and drinking and carousing, it's as if my Japanese friends and family have stumbled upon some advanced alien technology that puts them centuries ahead of the rest of us. They are walking encyclopedias of what's in season, how it must be prepared, and what you should drink with it. When it comes to dining out together, we always prefer places with a smooth and continuous relationship between food and drink that's exemplified by the *izakaya*—the Japanese pub. The izakaya takes a free-flowing approach to dinner that's thankfully becoming more and more common in the States, both in American izakayas and in restaurants that aren't nominally Japanese. At an izakaya, you might start your meal with a frosty beer and a scoop of potato salad, then proceed to sashimi with sake, followed by plates of grilled peppers and pork meatballs glazed in soy sauce tare, a glass of shochu, and, finally, a little bowl of noodles. Good Times is all about dishes that are conducive to sharing while you sip on an adult beverage.

New Year's: This section is a little bit of a wild card, but when I sat down to think about the things that defined my life in Japan, I couldn't get New Year's out of my head. Some of our best meals happened on New Year's, when we pulled out all the stops and dedicated a whole day to cooking and eating and drinking. In Japan, New Year's is when you reflect on the past year and show your appreciation for friends and family through food. You cook all the little symbolic snacks that will ensure prosperity in the coming year, then put in the effort of preparing a couple of showstopper dishes: a big prime rib, say, or a whole sea bream cooked in rice, or chicken breasts stuffed with root vegetables. New Year's is the most festive and important occasion of the year in Japan, but I find it doubly important because it represents the effect Japan has had on me. Truth be told, I was never a big fan of New Year's until I moved to Tokyo. Experiencing it from a Japanese perspective changed my mind completely about what the holiday could be. It's one of a hundred thousand things that make me grateful for Japan.

That's the lay of the land. I'm writing this book with my very good friend Chris Ying, with whom I wrote my first book, *Ivan Ramen*. Chris constantly moans and groans about how I call him on the phone too often, but obviously it's helped him understand the minute idiosyncrasies of my speech and translate them to the written page. You're welcome, Chris.

Jokes aside, Chris is a smart guy, a great writer, and the loving father of a young daughter. The true magic of our partnership is not that he can imitate my voice and tell my stories, but that we push one another to be better at what we do, whether it's writing, cooking, or raising a family. It was his idea to call this book *The Gaijin Cookbook*. He was the one who asked me to consider what it means to have spent my life as an outsider—something I've always been without really thinking about it. I think I'm pretty good at writing recipes and telling stories, but I need Chris to challenge me to be more helpful and efficient and clear. Most of the experiences and information in this book come from my head, but he has given it all meaning and utility. This book is written in the first person, but believe me, it's as much Chris's book as it is mine.

I think it's important to talk about the nature of our collaboration, because I don't want you to get the impression that Chris is simply speaking for me. That's not how things work. You can't ever fully inhabit someone else's perspective. I like to joke around and tell Chris, a lifelong Californian, that I'm more Japanese than he is Chinese, but at the end of the day, no matter how well I speak Japanese or cook Japanese food, I'm always going to be a white guy. I can't possibly know what it's like for him (or my wife or my kids) to look in the mirror and see an Asian person.

We live in a tricky time for anybody who wants to cook and sell food that comes from another person's culture. Perhaps we'll look back in twenty years and laugh about how bad we were at sharing our culinary traditions respectfully and responsibly. For now, I can only say that this book is called *The Gaijin Cookbook* because that's exactly what it is: a book written by two gaijin. It's not a dissertation on Japanese foodways. It's everything that a Jewish guy from New York has soaked up about Japanese food, distilled through the brain of my Chinese-American coauthor. Our first hope is that you'll get a lot of use out of this book, feeding your family and friends tasty Japanese dishes you've always wanted to know how to make, as well as a few things that are brand-new to you. But if we've done our jobs right, this book will also say a little something about having the humility and willingness to learn from one another.

A Few Words on Cookability

We really, truly want you to cook from this book. The recipes are not intended for professional restaurants—they come from our home kitchens and are aimed directly at yours.

Now perhaps you're saying, "But I live in a small, rural, racially homogeneous town without access to katsuobushi," or "I don't even know what katsuobushi is and I fear the unfamiliar." Well, don't fret. Toward the back of this book, there's a complete glossary of specialty ingredients (page 239), along with tips on where to find them and suggestions for common substitutes. In all honesty, the majority of the recipes in this book will be within reach once you place one online order or make one trip to an Asian market. It's worth it—but you already know that, or you wouldn't be reading this book.

The Recipes by Category

HOT POTS

NOODLES

PARTIES AND FUN FOR A CROWD

BAGELS AND SANDWICHES

ACCESSORIES

NOTE: V INDICATES VEGETARIAN DISHES OR ONES THAT
CAN EASILY BE MADE SO BY OMITTING AN INGREDIENT
OR SUBSTITUTING VEGETABLE DASHI.

Eat More Japanese

How the Hell Do I "Eat Japanese"?

First, let's be clear: There is no single Japanese way of eating. Japanese people do not think or eat as one. You might be excused for believing otherwise if your experience is based on restaurants in America, which tend to represent certain cuisines with the same templated menu (think about your typical moderately priced Vietnamese, Mexican, Thai, or Indian place). But the truth is, that says more about the people consuming than the people cooking. To eat more Japanese doesn't simply mean eating more sushi or more ramen.

Sure, there are ingredients that appear over and over again in Japanese cooking and dishes that are revered in Japan. But there are Japanese people who don't like sushi, just as there are Americans who don't like apple pie. When I suggest that you "eat more Japanese," I'm talking about cooking and dining according to Japanese ideals even when you're not eating classically Japanese food. It's about not only specific flavors and techniques, but also a set of principles I've learned over the years that govern how I feed my family: attention to detail, variety, and balanced umami. To me, eating more Japanese means that whether I'm making hot dogs or tacos or teriyaki, I keep my eye on these core values.

I find that eating more Japanese, besides being an outright tastier way of life, makes me a better, healthier cook for my family. In our house, we strive for a diverse range of tastes over large portions. The food we cook is deeply satisfying, owing to Japanese ingredients and ideas that accentuate umami. My kids have a better relationship with good, healthy food because we feed them things that are friendly to their palates—but not dumbed down. And my wife eats my cooking and feels a connection to the place where she was born and raised.

This chapter includes some of the canonical recipes and flavors of Japanese cooking, as well as an assortment of dishes that speak to the broader themes I'm talking about. Don't take this to be a definitive catalog. These are the recipes that have inspired and sustained me and my family throughout our lives in Japan, and now New York.

Before we get into it, though, let's take a quick run through the bigger ideas I'm encouraging you to consider.

The Devil Is in the Details

American chefs tend to view Japanese chefs with a sort of awestruck reverence. Not just the fancy sushi and kaiseki chefs, either. We're equally enamored of the street-level vendors and ramen shop owners, who have a proficiency in their work that seems far out of sync with the small amount of money they're charging. Much of their skill derives from the notion of *shokunin*—a word that translates roughly as "craftsmanship" but really implies mastery and a singular dedication to doing one thing really well. We'll deal with this concept more later in the book (see Otaku, page 141), but here I want to zoom in on one aspect of shokunin: attention to detail.

Doing the simple things well—rice and broth, for instance—is crucial, because the simple things are the backbone of good cooking. Unfortunately,

Top left: Scallops being steamed streetside in Tokyo.
Top right: Seiyoken, a super-classic *yoshoku* (Western-style) restaurant.
Bottom right: The illustrious *conbini* (Japanese convenience store).
Bottom left: Kayaba Coffee, an old-school coffee shop in Yanaka.

because the fundamentals aren't especially sexy, they're often treated as afterthoughts. But if your rice is shitty, it doesn't really matter what you put on top of it, does it? This is not a concept that's unique to Japanese food. Chris and I talk about it all the time. Have you ever had a Thai curry made with fresh coconut cream, rather than the canned stuff? It makes all the difference in the world. Or consider this: American hamburgers are the best because we have the best burger buns. Not the best beef or zaniest toppings. The best buns. Outside of the States, people tend to throw burger patties on whatever crusty bread they have on hand. Pay attention to the details, people.

A Little Bit of Everything

One night in Tokyo, my son Isaac invited a friend over for dinner. I made a roast chicken, some vegetables, and some rice. When I set the food on the table, Isaac's friend looked at it, and then over at me, as if to say, "Where's all the food?" I knew what he was thinking, because my wife has the same reaction whenever I cook a standard American meat + starch + veg meal: "That's so sad. Where's the pickle? Where's the simmered dish? Where's the color? There's nothing green or red or yellow. The food is all brown." Eventually she gives up and we eat, but I know she's only happy when dinner has six or seven components.

A good home-cooked dinner in Japan would include a medley of small dishes: simmered burdock root (gobo) with sea salt, perhaps; fresh tofu, fried and soaked in dashi, so it's crisp and gooey at the same time; a spoonful of grated daikon next to a piece of oily fish; a bowl of vegetables simmered in dashi and soy; a simple salad with a citrusy dressing. When I first moved to Tokyo, in the eighties, I lived on meals at the local *teishoku-ya* (diner). For not very much money, I'd sit down and have a full meal of miso soup, vegetables, pickles, rice, and fish or some other simple entrée. My goal is to eat like that all the time—little tastes of a lot of different things. Does that always happen at my house? Hell no. But we try.

Umami as a Balancing Act

A Japanese scientist named Kikunae Ikeda was the first person to assign a name to the elusive taste of savoriness. *Umami* is a portmanteau of the words *umai* (delicious) and *mi* (taste), which is a charmingly simple way of describing the unifying thread among tomatoes, beef, seaweed, mushrooms, kimchi, Parmesan cheese, miso, soy sauce, fish sauce, MSG, and breast milk. Umami is the taste of craving, although it's not necessarily a flavor on its own. As many cooks in Japan and around the world have discovered, umami works best in combination with other basic tastes.

At this point, umami is a well-known concept in America, but its usage is still misunderstood. Shinobu Namae, the chef of L'Effervescence, a two-Michelin-star restaurant in Tokyo, gives an incredible lecture about umami that uses the Big Mac as a prime example. It's not the umami in the beef that makes the Big Mac delicious, he explains. It's the interplay of umami with the sweetness from the ketchup and bun, salt, fat from the cheese and sauce, and acidity from the pickles.

In this book, we lean heavily on an umami-rich combination of shoyu (soy sauce), mirin, sake, sugar, and katsuobushi (bonito flakes). Once you taste it, you'll probably recognize it from various Japanese dishes you've had over the years, and you'll see it here over and over in different ratios. In addition to being the ideal balance of sweet, salty, smoky, and umami, it's the taste of home to me.

Japanese at Heart

I know I started out by saying that eating more Japanese wasn't about specific dishes, but that doesn't mean there aren't specifically Japanese tastes and textures.

Take natto, for instance. Natto is a comically sticky-slimy, funky-pungent product made from fermented soybeans. It's part of a family of foods

I regrettably didn't catch the name of this woman running a yakitori stand near Kappabashi, but she grilled the hell out of chicken.

Your everyday fish market in Tokyo. Swoon.

with textures that challenge Americans, like mountain yam, sea cucumber, jellyfish, aspic, tripe, and chicken feet. If it's not something you grew up eating, chances are it will take you a long time to get used to it, and even longer to love it. I've included a few natto recipes in this chapter because it's something I've come to really adore, and I think it's worth trying to learn to love it. Remember that most Americans were turned off by raw fish until about thirty years ago.

Speaking of raw fish, it's impossible to talk about Japanese cooking without talking about seafood. Japan is an island, so seafood is an obvious resource. But Japanese seafood is not limited to sashimi and nigiri. The flavor of the sea is integrated into the cuisine in a multitude of interesting ways. Dashi, for example, the broth made of seaweed and smoked-and-dried fish, is at the heart of much of Japanese cooking, and there are dozens of different versions—everything from ones made with ultra-expensive artisanal kombu and an assortment of dried seafood to dashi tea bags to granulated instant dashi.

Throughout this chapter (and, in fact, this book), I've tried to demonstrate the multitude of ways that seafood—whether fish, shellfish, seaweed, or katsuobushi—sneaks into my home cooking. Even if you live in a landlocked part of the country, there are still creative methods of capturing the essence of the ocean without sacrificing that most Japanese of all cooking traits: using the freshest ingredients the season offers.

How to Cook a Pot of Japanese Rice

Makes about 4 cups

Rice is too often overlooked.

If you're like me, you've probably suffered through dinner at a friend's home (or maybe even your own home) where the food was great in general, but the rice was under- or overcooked. Or perhaps you've visited one of America's many-splendored pan-Asian restaurants, where you were served Japanese dishes with jasmine rice or some other incongruous variety. Immediately you sensed something was amiss—like seeing a perfect slice of jamón Ibérico served on top of a saltine.

The dishes in this book are best made or eaten with plump short-grain rice. Medium- and long-grain rices have their place in Chinese, Southeast Asian, Indian, and Cajun cooking, but Japanese food just doesn't play well with fluffy, aromatic rice varieties. At least that's what I've found. (Thank god this is a book and not a social media post, or I'm sure the comments section would be lighting up right now with people telling me how ignorant and racist I am.)

As far as cooking rice goes, there are dozens of ways to do it. You can use an electric rice cooker, obviously. Rice that's cooked in a *donabe* (clay pot) comes out exceptionally well, perfectly chewy and evenly cooked. At my house, I use a 1½-quart enamel-coated cast-iron pot made by Staub. Like a donabe, it's beautiful, so you can take it straight to the table. I know that some people swear by those newfangled all-in-one pressure cooker/rice cooker/slow cooker/laundry/ photocopy machines, but I haven't had the best luck with them. Granted, it might simply come down to adjusting my method. Each style of rice cookery uses a different ratio of water to rice (e.g., 1.25:1 in an electric rice cooker and closer to 1:1 in a donabe or cast-iron pot). For generations, cooks around the world have sworn by the knuckle method of measuring water, where you touch the tip of your finger to the rice and add water up to your first knuckle. Over time you might get comfortable enough with your equipment to measure this way. However, using exact measurements means you'll get perfect rice every time.

The following instructions are based on the 1½-quart rice pot I have, but you can use the same basic method with a donabe or even a heavy-bottomed saucepan. You'll likely have to make some adjustments to the amount of water and the cooking time, but it's absolutely worth the effort to dial in your routine and keep track of what works best for you.

1½ cups Japanese short-grain rice (320 grams, to be exact)

1. Place the rice in a fine-mesh strainer and rinse under cold water, using your fingers to agitate the rice, until the water runs almost clear. (Alternatively, place the rice in a pot or bowl and rinse and drain away the water three times.)

2. Add the rice to a 1½-quart enamel-glazed cast-iron pot (or similarly sized heavy saucepan) and cover with 1½ cups (345 grams, if you want to weigh it) cold water. Let the rice soak for at least 20 minutes or up to 1 hour.

3. Bring the water to a simmer over medium-high heat, stirring a few times to prevent the rice from clumping or sticking. Once the water's simmering, cover the pot and turn the heat down to low. Set a timer for 14 minutes. After 14 minutes, turn off the heat and let the rice sit for 5 minutes before uncovering and fluffing it with a spoon or spatula. Serve within an hour.

Sushi Rice

Makes about 4 cups

When Americans sit down for sushi, we tend to fixate on the fish (and the toppings on the fish), but to ignore the rice is to ignore half the meal. The very best sushi chefs I've encountered in Japan are fastidious about the type of rice they use, when it was harvested, how they rinse it, how long they cook it, what they use to season it, and what temperature it is when they serve it. The cumulative effect of all these details is obvious and dramatic.

To me, having perfectly cooked rice is more important than what you use to season it. Many recipes instruct you to season sushi rice with mirin (sweet cooking wine), while others insist on using aka-zu (aged red vinegar made from the mash left from sake-making). I keep things pretty simple with sugar, salt, and rice vinegar.

4 cups freshly steamed rice
  (page 25)
3 tablespoons rice vinegar
2 tablespoons sugar
1 tablespoon kosher salt

Place the rice in a bowl. Combine the vinegar, sugar, and salt in a separate bowl and whisk to dissolve. Pour the mixture over the hot rice a little bit at a time, gently turning and mixing the rice with a spoon or rice paddle. Cover the rice with a damp cloth and serve within an hour.

The view from the bar at Fujisei, a sushi restaurant in Azabujuban, one of Tokyo's tonier neighborhoods.

Dashi

Makes about 7 cups

Dashi is one of the foundational building blocks of Japanese cooking. It's an extremely useful, lightly smoky, umami-filled broth made from seaweed (kombu) and flakes of smoked, dried bonito (katsuobushi). But there are as many variations on dashi as there are cooks making it. You can change up the kind of seaweed or dried seafood you use, and you can make infinite tweaks to the temperature of the water and the length of time you let things soak. I'm guilty of being extremely fussy about dashi, especially in a restaurant context. But this recipe is for a quick utilitarian dashi, meant for busy home cooks.

I'm not inventing anything new here, and I don't think I'm being sacrilegious. Plenty of Japanese cookbooks suggest shortcuts like omitting the seaweed entirely (see Katsuo Dashi, below), and in Japan, a lot of home cooks use dashi packets, which function like savory tea bags. If you can get your hands on some, I highly recommend them too. Lastly, I've also included a katsuobushi-free vegetable-based dashi recipe that should make it easy to convert many of the recipes in this book into vegetarian versions.

One 5-x-10-inch sheet kombu

4 cups tightly packed katsuobushi (bonito flakes)

1. Bring 8 cups water to a bare simmer in a large saucepan, then shut off the heat and add the kombu. Let the seaweed sit for 5 minutes, then add the katsuobushi, cover the pan, and allow to soak for 15 more minutes.

2. Strain the broth through a fine-mesh strainer and let cool. Use immediately, or pack up and store. The dashi will keep for 2 days covered in the fridge or for a couple months if you freeze it into ice cubes and store them in a zip-top bag with the air squeezed out.

Katsuo Dashi

Makes about 3 cups

A very smoky, very delicious dashi that you can make if you don't have any kombu on hand.

2½ cups tightly packed katsuobushi (bonito flakes)

1. Bring 4 cups water to a bare simmer in a medium saucepan, then shut off the heat. Let the water cool for about a minute, then add the katsuobushi, cover the pan, and leave to soak for 15 minutes.

2. Strain the broth through a fine-mesh strainer and use immediately, or store for 2 days, covered, in the fridge. Or freeze into ice cubes and store in a zip-top bag for up to a couple months.

Vegetable Dashi

Makes about 8 cups

While it lacks the smokiness of regular dashi, this katsuobushi-less dashi can step in admirably in any dish that you want to keep vegetarian.

8 dried shiitake mushrooms

¼ cup vegetable oil

1 large onion, roughly chopped

½ head green cabbage, roughly chopped

2 bunches scallions, cut into 1-inch lengths

1 large carrot, roughly chopped

1 russet potato, peeled and roughly chopped

6 garlic cloves, peeled

2 teaspoons kosher salt

One 5-inch square kombu

Discussing the merits of various types of katsuobushi (bonito flakes) at a shop in Kichijoji.

1. Place the dried shiitakes in a small bowl and cover with 1 cup warm water. Allow to soak for 30 minutes.

2. Heat a medium pot over medium-high heat and add the vegetable oil. Add the onion, cabbage, scallions, carrot, potato, and garlic and sprinkle with the salt.

Cook, stirring regularly, for 3 to 4 minutes, or until the vegetables have softened slightly and given up some of their liquid. Add 9 cups water along with the shiitakes and their soaking liquid, and the kombu, and bring to a gentle simmer, then lower the heat and simmer very gently for 1 hour.

3. Remove the pot from the heat and strain the dashi through a fine-mesh strainer. Use immediately or allow to cool to room temperature, then transfer to airtight containers and store in the fridge for up to 4 days. Vegetable dashi also keeps well for a couple months, frozen into ice cubes and stored in a zip-top bag.

Eggs

Two Ways

When I'm in America, I'm not much of an egg guy, but whenever I land in Japan, I immediately find myself eating eggs by the dozen. I'll take them however I can get them, whether in omelets, egg salad, or soup; ajitama (perfectly soft-boiled eggs marinated in sweetened soy sauce); raw eggs on rice; or onsen tamago. Named for the natural hot springs (*onsen*) located all around Japan, onsen tamago are eggs that were traditionally poached slowly in the consistently warm waters of the springs, so that when you cracked open the shells, the yolks were perfectly creamy while the whites were soft and jelly-like.

Both onsen tamago and ajitama are dead simple to make and keep for a few days in the fridge. From there they can find multiple paths into dinner, whether you drop an onsen tamago into a bowl of ramen or Beef and Onion Rice Bowl (Gyudon, page 125), or simmer ajitama in a pot of Oden (page 146), or smash one into a bowl of rice.

Hot-Spring Eggs (Onsen Tamago)

Makes 4 eggs

These days, poaching eggs in hot springs has been made somewhat irrelevant by sous vide machines, but since most of us have neither a volcanic spring nor a water circulator at home, here's a recipe designed for the average home kitchen.

4 large eggs, left to sit at room temperature for 30 minutes

Bring 6 cups water to a full boil in a small heavy saucepan, then shut off the heat and add 1 cup cold water. Gently lower the eggs into the pan with a slotted spoon or strainer and allow them to sit for 12 to 13 minutes. You're trying for eggs that look like they've been perfectly poached, with runny yolks and jiggly whites. (You may have to make a test-run batch to get the timing just right.) Lift out the eggs and immediately plunge them into an ice bath to chill for a few minutes. Store in the fridge for up to 2 days. When you're ready to use them, crack the eggs open as you would raw ones.

Soy-Marinated Eggs (Ajitama)

Makes 5 eggs

5 large eggs
1 cup mirin
1 cup sake
1 cup soy sauce
2 tablespoons sugar
½ cup tightly packed katsuobushi (bonito flakes)

1. Bring a medium saucepan of water to a boil. Carefully lower in the eggs with a slotted spoon or strainer and cook for 7 minutes and 15 seconds (set a timer), then immediately lift them out and plunge into an ice bath. Let the eggs cool completely.

2. Meanwhile, bring the mirin, sake, soy sauce, and sugar to a simmer in a saucepan, stirring to dissolve the sugar. Shut off the heat and add the katsuobushi. Allow to steep for 10 minutes, then strain and cool the liquid.

3. Crack and peel the eggs and place in a large zip-top bag. Add the cooled liquid and seal. Refrigerate for a minimum of 12 hours before serving. After 24 hours, remove the eggs from the brine and store in the fridge for up to a few days longer.

Soy-Marinated Tuna (Maguro Zuke)

Serves 4 as part of a larger meal

If you asked a hundred different Americans to talk about Japanese food, I'm certain that every one of them would mention raw fish. Many people assume that eating Japanese food means eating raw fish. But here's the thing: At the core of Japanese cooking—hell, all good cooking really—is the idea of using the ingredients around you. Japan is an island nation, so access to staggeringly fresh seafood is a natural part of the culinary culture. Part of the reason our ocean stocks are depleted is that people think they should be able to eat sushi and sashimi wherever they are, whenever they want. In other words, if you're reading this book in a landlocked part of the world where fish has to be frozen and flown to your grocery store, maybe skip this recipe. There are plenty of other things in here for you to make.

But if you live in a place where high-quality fresh tuna is available, this is a quick and easy treatment that you can give it before serving the fish over a bowl of steamed rice or as part of a Temaki Party (page 64) or Family-Style Chirashi (page 197). Marinating tuna in soy sauce both draws water out and pulls flavor into the meat via osmosis. The flesh will firm up a bit and gain tons of umami.

8 ounces fresh tuna
¾ cup soy sauce
½ cup sake
½ cup mirin

1. Slice the tuna thin, as you would for sashimi. (If that means nothing to you, have a look online.) Alternatively, feel free to dice the tuna into small chunks.

2. Mix the soy sauce, sake, and mirin together in a bowl. Place the tuna in a single layer in a small container and pour the marinade on top. Allow to soak for 30 minutes, flipping the slices halfway through.

3. Serve immediately, or discard the liquid and wrap the fish in plastic. It will keep in the fridge overnight.

Squid in Butter-Soy Sauce (Ika Butter Yaki)

Serves 4 as an appetizer

Butter and soy sauce. If this combination isn't already in your everyday cooking repertoire, it should be, right alongside salt and pepper, fish sauce and lime, and peanut butter and chocolate. It's a super-flexible pairing that simultaneously brings richness, umami, and salt to a dish. Here I'm employing it in a standard izakaya (Japanese pub) preparation of sautéed squid, but it works equally well with mushrooms, greens, potatoes, pasta, chicken, scallops, or fish. On special occasions, I'll sear a thick two-pound rib-eye steak in a cast-iron pan, then pop it in the oven to finish. When it's a few minutes shy of medium-rare, I top it with a big pat of butter and good glug of soy. The butter bastes the steak, then mingles with the steak juices and soy in the pan to make a perfect sauce.

1 pound cleaned squid

3 tablespoons unsalted butter

1 garlic clove, minced

1 tablespoon soy sauce

GARNISH

Scallion greens, sliced on the bias

1. Be sure to remove the cartilage and beaks from the squid—look it up online if you're not sure how to do it. Cut the squid bodies into ½-inch-wide rings and dry them with a paper towel. Leave the tentacles whole.

2. Heat a large skillet over medium heat, then add the butter and swirl to melt it and coat the pan. Butter can burn quickly, so don't take your eyes off it. As soon as the melted butter begins to foam, stir in the garlic and cook for about a minute, until the pungency of the raw garlic recedes, then add the squid. Toss and stir the squid until just cooked, no more than a couple minutes, then add the soy sauce and cook until the soy and butter meld into a uniform sauce, about a minute.

3. Top the squid with scallion greens and serve immediately, preferably with ice-cold beer.

Cold Udon with Dipping Broth (Bukkake Udon)

Serves 2

The Japanese word *bukkake* translates to something like "splash with." Unfortunately, it's a term that has been completely co-opted by porn, and no matter how many times I say it, it never fails to elicit a giggle from my juvenile coauthor, Chris.

There are two basic elements here: noodles and dipping broth. The noodles can be either udon or soba, depending on your preference. As all great pasta cultures have discovered, a lot rides on the quality of your noodles. Buy the best-quality you can find.

The broth is the epitome of the sweet, salty, and lightly smoky flavor profile generated by combining soy sauce, mirin, sake, and katsuobushi. If you've had this dish before, you can probably recall the taste of the broth with very little effort. And, as I mentioned in the introduction to this chapter, you'll see different versions of this combination throughout the book.

More often than not with bukkake udon, the broth is served separately from the noodles, allowing you to dip and slurp them one mouthful at a time. I'm a big fan of dipping noodles—when the noodles are ramen, this is called *tsukemen*—but I also really like this one-bowl approach. It's convenient, and there are fewer dishes to wash later.

Kosher salt

10 ounces dried udon (or soba)

½ cup finely grated daikon

2 large egg yolks (of a quality
and freshness that you feel
comfortable eating raw)

¼ cup chopped scallions

½ cup tightly packed katsuobushi
(bonito flakes)

1½ cups Dipping Broth (Tsuketsuyu,
recipe follows), chilled

FOR SERVING

Wasabi paste (from a tube is fine;
optional)

1. Bring a pot of water to a boil and season generously with salt. Meanwhile, set up an ice bath with plenty of ice and water, as you want your noodles thoroughly chilled.

2. Cook the noodles according to the package instructions. Drain and plunge into the ice bath. Give them a stir with your fingers or a pair of chopsticks and allow to cool for a minute or two. Pull the noodles out of the ice bath, deposit them in a strainer, and give them a good shake to get rid of as much water as possible, then divide between two bowls.

3. Top each serving of noodles with a big spoonful of daikon. Use the back of the spoon to press a little crater into the daikon in each bowl, then nest an egg yolk in it. Sprinkle the scallions on top and tuck a pile of katsuobushi into each bowl. Pour half the dipping broth into each, garnish with a dab of wasabi if you like, and serve immediately.

Dipping Broth (Tsuketsuyu)

Makes 3 cups

1½ cups Dashi (page 28)

½ cup sake

½ cup mirin

½ cup soy sauce

1 tablespoon sugar

Whisk everything together in a bowl to dissolve the sugar. Store in an airtight container in the fridge for up to 3 days. Give it a vigorous shake or stir before serving.

THE VANISHING JAPANESE DINER
[TEISHOKU-YA]

Teishoku-ya are basically the Japanese equivalent of an American diner—places where you go to have reliable meals that include classic dishes everybody is familiar with. When I moved to Tokyo straight out of college, I ate almost exclusively at these places. They were ubiquitous, cheap, and ideal for someone like me who wanted to experience everyday Japanese dining in its purest form. I'd get a crisp piece of broiled mackerel, a bowl of rice, a little plate of daikon pickles (takuan), a decent miso soup, and maybe one other little vegetable side for around six bucks.

These days, the independently owned charming teishoku-ya of my memories are becoming less common in Japan. But the dishes I first tasted in those halcyon days are alive and well in my own kitchen, making regular appearances at our family dinners. With a bowl of rice and miso soup, any of the five recipes that follow will make a well-rounded meal, whether you're a clueless recent college grad or a parent trying to feed your family on a weekday evening.

Miso-Braised Mackerel (Saba Misoni)

Serves 2

Many Americans shy away from oily, shiny-skinned fish like mackerel and sardines in favor of the milder flavors of salmon and cod. But I grew up eating bluefish in New York and became a regular sushi eater as a teenager, so I fell in love early with the strong flavors of oily fish. To me, a really fresh piece of mackerel at a sushi bar is almost preferable to fatty tuna. It's so implanted in our brains that we're supposed to swoon at toro, but honestly, how much fatty tuna can you really stomach before you start feeling ill? On the other hand, I could sit at the bar and eat piece after piece of *saba* (mackerel), *sanma* (Japanese pike), and *iwashi* (sardine). This recipe is for a simmered mackerel preparation that you'll find at any teishoku-ya, served with warm rice, miso soup, and some pickles.

2 very fresh skin-on mackerel fillets (about 12 ounces)
¼ cup white (shiro) miso
2 tablespoons soy sauce
2 tablespoons mirin
2 tablespoons sake
1½ teaspoons sugar
One 1-inch piece ginger, sliced thin

FOR SERVING
Steamed rice (page 25)

1. Using a sharp knife or a razor blade, score a shallow 1-inch X into the skin side of each mackerel fillet to prevent them from curling up as they cook. Place the fillets in a heatproof bowl or container.

2. Bring ½ cup water to a simmer in a small saucepan, then pour over the mackerel fillets. Use a pair of chopsticks to stir the fillets around for 30 seconds to render and remove some of the fat and fishier flavors. Transfer the fillets to a small skillet or saucepan that holds them relatively snugly in a single layer.

3. Combine the miso, soy, mirin, sake, and sugar with ¼ cup water in a bowl and whisk to combine. Add the ginger, then pour over the mackerel fillets and set the pan over medium heat. If you happen to have a lid that is slightly too small for your pan, use it to cover the fillets and press them down into the liquid. If not, use a regular lid and leave the pan slightly uncovered. Bring the liquid to a gentle simmer, lower the heat, and cook for 10 minutes, flipping the fish over halfway through.

4. Transfer the mackerel to plates and top with the sauce. Serve with steamed rice.

Panfried Pork Cutlets in Ginger Sauce (Shogayaki)

Serves 4

This is another of the dishes I first encountered at one of Tokyo's many teishoku-ya back in the eighties. Fast-forward three decades, and shogayaki is one of the dishes that we make most often at home—at least three or four times a month. It has a flavor that kids understand—sweet, with just a tickle of spice from the ginger—and it's a perfect foil for a bowl of white rice. Any leftover pork cutlets reheat perfectly the next day.

We've played around with a lot of shogayaki recipes through the years. My wife, Mari, will be at her friend's house and notice that she makes it a certain way, and for a few months we'll do it that way too. This version is the one we're currently enamored of, but feel free to adjust as you see fit, using more ginger or making it less sweet or saltier.

1¾ pounds pork tenderloin
   (or 12 thin pork cutlets)
One 3-inch piece ginger, peeled
   and minced or grated
½ cup soy sauce
½ cup sake
¼ cup mirin
2 tablespoons sugar
½ cup all-purpose flour
About ½ cup vegetable oil
1 large onion, sliced thin
½ teaspoon kosher salt

FOR SERVING
Steamed rice (page 25)

1. Slice the tenderloin into 12 pieces of equal size. (If you have presliced cutlets, move on to step 2.) Working with one at a time, cover each piece with a sheet of plastic wrap and use a meat mallet or rolling pin to pound it into a flat cutlet about ¼ inch thick. Don't brutalize the meat—ten to twelve moderately firm whacks ought to do it.

2. Whisk together the ginger, soy sauce, sake, mirin, and sugar in a bowl. Put the flour in a separate bowl.

3. Heat a large skillet over medium-high heat, then coat with 2 tablespoons of the vegetable oil. Working in batches, dredge the cutlets in flour, shake off the excess, and cook until they're lightly browned, about 3 minutes on each side, then transfer to a plate. Add more oil to the pan as necessary to keep successive batches from sticking, and don't worry about cooking the meat all the way through—it'll finish in the sauce.

4. Lower the heat to medium and add the onion to the pan. Season with the salt and cook, stirring often, until the onion has wilted and begun to brown, about 6 minutes. Remove and set aside.

5. Pour the sauce mixture into the pan and use a spatula to dislodge any browned bits stuck to the bottom. Pile the browned cutlets back in—it's fine if they overlap and stack up. Cover the pork with the cooked onion and bring the sauce to a simmer, shaking the pan and wiggling things around to make sure all of the cutlets come into contact with sauce. Drop the heat to medium-low and cook until the sauce thickens slightly, about 3 minutes. Serve with steamed rice.

Teriyaki Yellowtail (Buri no Teriyaki)

Serves 4 as part of a larger meal

Gaijin love yellowtail. It's a fish that's mild in flavor and fatty, and it's a mainstay at every sushi bar in America. For this preparation—another standard at any Japanese diner—I sear fillets of yellowtail (called hamachi or buri, depending on the size and species) in a hot pan, then simmer them in sake, mirin, and soy sauce. The fat renders from the fish and mingles with the liquid, creating a surprisingly rich sauce.

4 yellowtail (hamachi) fillets
  (about 12 ounces)
1½ teaspoons kosher salt
3 tablespoons sake
3 tablespoons mirin
3 tablespoons soy sauce
1 tablespoon plus 2 teaspoons
  sugar
2 teaspoons vegetable oil

FOR SERVING
Steamed rice (page 25)

1. Pat the yellowtail fillets dry with a paper towel, then season lightly with the salt. Set aside.

2. Whisk together the sake, mirin, soy sauce, and sugar in a bowl.

3. Heat a large nonstick skillet over medium heat, then coat with the vegetable oil. Carefully lay the yellowtail fillets in the pan and cook until golden brown on the first side, about 2 minutes. Flip and cook for 1 more minute. Add the sauce mixture and cook for about 3 minutes, flipping the fillets occasionally to coat them in sauce, until the fish is cooked through and the sauce is beginning to get syrupy.

4. Transfer the fillets to a plate and top with the sauce. Serve with steamed rice.

Chicken and Egg Bowl (Oyakodon)

Serves 4 to 6

Oyakodon is one of the giants of Japanese cuisine. *Oyako* translates literally as "parent-child," and the name refers to the dish's two main ingredients: chicken and egg. To make oyakodon, you poach chicken thighs in dashi with a little onion, then mix in eggs to create an unbelievably fluffy custard-sauce.

Yakitori restaurants always have oyakodon on the menu, as do most teishoku-ya. And here in the States, you can make oyakodon at home with very little trouble.

1 cup Dashi (page 28)

½ cup mirin

¼ cup plus 1 tablespoon soy sauce

14 ounces boneless, skinless chicken thighs, cut into 1-inch chunks

½ onion, sliced very thin

2 scallions, sliced thin on the bias

12 large eggs, lightly beaten

FOR SERVING

Steamed rice (page 25)

Shichimi togarashi

Ground sansho pepper (optional)

1. Combine the dashi, mirin, and soy sauce in a large skillet and bring to a gentle simmer over medium heat. Add the chicken and cook until it's halfway done, about 2 minutes. Add the onion and scallions and cook for 2 to 3 minutes, or until the vegetables have softened and the chicken is cooked through.

2. Drop the heat to medium-low and slowly trickle the beaten eggs into the pan, stirring slowly in a circular motion with chopsticks or a wooden spoon. The timing will probably be 2 to 3 minutes, but this takes a little bit of finesse to get exactly right—you want the eggs to be more custard than curd, which is a fine line. Err on the side of less cooked, and you will be rewarded with an eggy-dashi-chickeny sauce.

3. Serve the oyakodon over bowls of steamed rice and garnish with togarashi and/or sansho pepper. Eat with spoons.

Fried Pork Cutlets (Tonkatsu)

Serves 4

If, for some baffling reason, you have this book but aren't sure you like Japanese food, this recipe is for you. Maybe you're a grumpy dad whose college-age kids bought you the book as part of their ongoing campaign to break you free of your old habits. But you *like* your habits, damn it. You were interested in being cool when you were twenty-three, but you know what? It's exhausting. You like meat and potatoes, and if they're fried, all the better. Well, sir, here you go: crunchy breaded pork tenderloin with tangy Japanese Bull-Dog tonkatsu sauce. If you don't want to eat the cabbage on the side, fine by me.

Of course, in Japan, tonkatsu is not as lowbrow as I'm making it sound. On our last trip to Tokyo, Chris and I fell in love with a tonkatsu restaurant where every element of the meal was meticulously thought out. Rather than pounded pork cutlets, they offered us a choice of a variety of thick cuts of fatty pork: shoulder, loin, tenderloin, belly. Then the chef spent a solid minute carefully dusting the pork in flour and wiping off the excess so that it was a perfectly uniform coating. From there, he swirled it in a rich yellow egg wash and crusted it with feathery panko bread crumbs. The panko, of course, was made in-house, because the chef wasn't happy with anything he could buy.

This recipe is closer to grumpy-dad food—it's quick and uncomplicated, so you can get it on the table before Pops starts grumbling. But if you want to experiment with different cuts of pork, bread crumbs, and methods, more power to you. (For more on the high art of frying, see page 157.)

One 1-pound pork tenderloin
2 teaspoons kosher salt
½ cup all-purpose flour
1 large egg
¾ cup panko
1 cup vegetable oil

FOR SERVING
Steamed rice (page 25)
Shredded cabbage
Lemon wedges
Bull-Dog tonkatsu sauce

1. Slice the pork tenderloin crosswise into 4 equal pieces. Working with one piece at a time, place the pork, cut side down, on a cutting board and cover it loosely with plastic wrap. Use a meat mallet or rolling pin to pound the meat into a flat cutlet about ½ inch thick. Don't brutalize the meat—ten to twelve moderately firm whacks ought to do it. Season the cutlets lightly on both sides with the salt.

2. Set up a breading station by lining up three shallow pans—pie tins work well—and filling them with the flour, egg, and panko, respectively. Lightly beat the egg. One at a time, coat each piece of pork with flour, gently dusting off any excess, then give it a dip in egg and, finally, a coating of panko. Don't be stingy with the bread crumbs—cover the whole piece of meat and press down gently to ensure a good coating. Transfer to a plate.

3. Add the oil to a large skillet and heat over medium-high heat to 325°F. As a rough guide, the oil is ready when you drop a few pieces of panko in the oil and they immediately sizzle. Fry the cutlets in batches for 3 to 4 minutes per side, or until golden brown, then transfer to a wire rack and let rest for a few minutes.

4. Slice the pork into ½-inch-wide strips and serve with steamed rice, a big pile of shredded cabbage, lemon wedges, and a heavy drizzle of Bull-Dog sauce.

Pork Cutlets and Eggs over Rice (Katsudon)

Serves 4 to 6

Once your picky dad has been convinced by fried pork cutlets (see opposite) that maybe Japanese food isn't so bad after all, you can level him up to katsudon: pork cutlets nestled in a custardy pillow of eggs and onion seasoned with dashi and soy sauce.

1 tablespoon vegetable oil

1 onion, sliced thin

¾ cup Dashi (page 28)

⅓ cup mirin

¼ cup soy sauce

1 tablespoon sugar

10 large eggs, beaten

Fried Pork Cutlets (Tonkatsu, opposite), just cooked and cut into ½-inch-wide strips

FOR SERVING

Steamed rice (page 25)

Shichimi togarashi

1. Heat a large skillet over medium heat, then coat with the oil. Add the onion and cook for 3 to 4 minutes to get rid of some of the rawness. Add the dashi, mirin, soy, and sugar, bring to a gentle simmer, and cook for 4 to 5 minutes, or until the onion is tender.

2. Pour the beaten eggs into the pan and stir, scraping the pan with a rubber spatula to prevent them from setting on the bottom before they have a chance to cook on top.

As the eggs begin to get nice and custardy but aren't fully set, nestle in the pork slices. They'll lose some of their crispness, but the eggs will set around the pork in a soft nest. Serve over steamed rice, garnished with togarashi. (Alternatively, if you prefer that your tonkatsu stay slightly crisper, you can lay the pork slices directly onto your rice and then pour the custardy egg on top as a sort of sauce.)

Miso Soup

Serves 4

There are hundreds of paths to miso soup that vary according to how you make your dashi, the type of miso you prefer, and the ratio of the two. But at the end of the day, making miso soup is a stupid-simple procedure. I hesitate to even include a recipe in this book, because besides the fact that it's just miso and broth, you can buy pastes and powders that dissolve in hot water for decent miso soup. But since miso soup is essential to the teishoku-ya experience, I'm not going to make you chase down a recipe elsewhere.

I prefer a milder, sweeter miso, like shiro (white), for soup. If you've got something a little stronger in your fridge—red or yellow miso—start with a little less than what the recipe calls for and let your taste buds be your guide.

5 cups Dashi (page 28)

⅓ cup white (shiro) miso, or to taste

½ package (7 ounces) soft tofu, sliced into 1-inch cubes

¼ cup dried wakame (seaweed), soaked in cold water for 10 minutes and drained

FOR SERVING

5 scallions, sliced thin

1. Bring the dashi to a simmer in a saucepan, then scoop one large ladleful of the warm broth into a bowl and add the miso. Use a whisk to thoroughly dissolve the miso, then stir the mixture back into the pan. Give it a taste. If you think it could use more miso, add a little more to the bowl and repeat the whisk-and-incorporate procedure.

2. Add the tofu and soaked wakame and bring the broth to a simmer again. Give the soup one more gentle stir, divide among bowls, and top with the scallions.

Mari and I sharing miso soup and a host of teishoku-ya dishes at Mizuguchi Shokudo in the Asakusa district of Tokyo.

NATTO
[FERMENTED SOYBEANS]

It took me twenty-five years to fall in love with natto. For most of that time, I was put off by the texture. If you grew up associating sliminess with aliens, it's really difficult to see a bowl of natto as something you want to eat. Natto's flavor takes some getting used to as well, but if you like stinky cheese, you're basically already there.

After my first unhappy encounter with a gummy mass of fermented soybeans, I persevered, and I hope you do too. I've come to love natto. I mean that. It's not something I tolerate so I can appear credibly Japanese. I really do love it, and it only happened after I spent years of trying it. I've learned to appreciate its unique texture as something that you just don't get in Western cuisines—it's creamy without being fatty, gooey but not slippery. The flavor is extraordinarily savory and nuanced in a way that only fermentation can create. Nowadays a bowl of warm rice with natto is my breakfast on many mornings, but it's great

in lots of other dishes too, as you'll see in the following section. My kids grew up eating it, so they're down with natto in all its forms.

When you buy natto, it usually comes refrigerated, packed in small portions in plastic or Styrofoam. More often than not, the packages will include tiny packets of tare (seasoning sauce) and mustard. To achieve maximum natto-ness, you need to mix the sauces in with the natto and whip it until it's creamy-foamy. My rule of thumb is to whip it between 100 and 150 strokes with a pair of chopsticks, but some sticklers will tell you that nothing short of 400 will do.

Fermented Soybeans
with Tuna and Squid (Maguro Natto)

Serves 4

This is a gateway natto dish. It's still gooey and slimy—there's no avoiding that—but there's such a variety of flavors and textures here that the funk of the natto becomes more of a bass line than the primary melody.

I first had this dish at a little izakaya in Tokyo during my first stint in Japan. Atop a warm bowl of rice was a generous amount of raw fish mixed with whipped natto, sliced shiso leaves, cucumber, and pickles. It was bright and lively and undeniably delicious. Even if I didn't fall in love with natto at that moment, I got the sense that we might be right for each other.

Five 40-gram packages natto (fermented soybeans), with the included sauces

1 large egg (of a quality and freshness that you feel comfortable eating raw)

4 ounces very fresh tuna, diced small

3 ounces cleaned fresh squid, diced small

¼ cup finely diced cucumber

2 tablespoons diced takuan (pickled daikon)

4 shiso leaves, cut into ribbons

2 scallions, sliced thin

FOR SERVING
Steamed rice (page 25)
Soy sauce

1. Empty the packages of natto into a bowl. If the natto came with little pouches of tare (seasoning sauce) and mustard, add them to the bowl as well. Use a fork or a pair of chopsticks to whip the natto until it's fluffy and foamy—100 to 150 quick circles with the utensil of your choice.

2. Add the egg to the bowl and whip another 50 times. Stir in the tuna, squid, cucumber, takuan, shiso, and scallions. Scoop the mixture over bowls of warm steamed rice and serve immediately, with soy sauce on the side for seasoning.

Eggplant with Fermented Soybeans and Cilantro (Nasu Natto)

Serves 4 as part of a larger meal

For most of my marriage, I lived as an expat in Japan, but when Mari and I moved back to the States a few years ago, our roles reversed. My wife is an extremely capable and adaptable woman, but the change has been dramatic and sometimes very difficult. She pines for her home country and longs to feel connected to the things going on there. She keeps up with food trends in Japan and often asks me to try out new dishes for her. After reading about this particular combination of eggplant, natto, and cilantro from several sources, we gave it a whirl. I'm glad we did.

The sticky viscosity of the fermented soybeans melds seamlessly with the meaty-creamy texture of the eggplant. Their deep, earthy flavors complement each other as well, and the cilantro lifts everything up with its aromatic, citrusy pop.

Two 40-gram packages natto (fermented soybeans), with the included sauces

2 Japanese eggplants, cut into ½-inch dice

1 tablespoon vegetable oil

Leaves from ½ large bunch cilantro, chopped (¼ cup)

1 tablespoon soy sauce

1 teaspoon kosher salt

FOR SERVING

Japanese chili oil (rayu) or Chunky Chili Oil (page 234; optional)

1 Hot-Spring Egg (Onsen Tamago, page 30; optional)

Steamed rice (page 25)

1. Empty the packages of natto into a bowl. If the natto came with little pouches of tare (seasoning sauce) and mustard, add them to the bowl as well. Use a fork or a pair of chopsticks to whip the natto until it's fluffy and foamy—100 to 150 quick circles with the utensil of your choice.

2. Working in batches if necessary, arrange the eggplant in a single layer on a microwave-safe plate, cover with a paper towel, and microwave for 2 minutes. This will pull some of the moisture out of the eggplant and help it brown more quickly. If you don't have a microwave (or are offended by them), go straight to step 3 and cook the eggplant for a few minutes longer.

3. Heat a large skillet over medium heat, then coat with the oil. Add the eggplant and cook, stirring occasionally, for 6 to 7 minutes, or until cooked through and lightly browned. Work in batches if necessary to avoid crowding the pan.

4. Add the eggplant to the bowl with the whipped natto and stir thoroughly to combine. Mix in the cilantro, soy sauce, and salt and transfer to a serving bowl. A drizzle of chili oil is optional but highly recommended. If you want to add an egg for a little more richness, use the back of a spoon to create a little well in the center of the nasu natto and break the egg into it. Serve with warm steamed rice.

FEEDING OUR KIDS

If you ask my kids what they miss most about Japan, they'll tell you it's the freedom. When we were living in Tokyo, by the time they were seven or eight years old, they were taking the train to school on their own. After school they'd get on their bicycles and ride to the park. Here in the States, my youngest son, Ren, plays on a football team that practices at the park down the street. It's only three hundred yards from my house, but I'm still uncomfortable letting him walk by himself. Not that it's dangerous; it's more a matter of avoiding our neighbors' judgment. I don't want to get looks from other parents, or receive a call from the police about a lost half-Asian kid.

It's challenging to raise children with feet in two different cultures, but I think teaching my sons to be worldly people is one of the most important things I can do as a parent. I want my boys to connect with the best aspects of both Japan and the United States, and to feel proud of their dual heritage. And I want them to feel responsible and empowered to do the right things—including eating well. Sometimes it's about meeting them halfway, and other times it's about trusting them to have good taste.

Like every other family, we sometimes struggle to get the kids to eat a well-rounded diet. The upside of being a multicultural family is that our tool set is twice as big. In Japan, some industrious parents wake up early to make bento boxes that are full of variety and whimsy. They'll fry chicken, slice tomatoes, boil eggs, cook spinach and carrots, and steam rice, then use the ingredients to construct edible scenes: Pokémon and Disney and Dragonball. That's a little bit too crazy for me (although Mari has tried it a few times), but the general idea still holds.

Kids need to feel that food is a source of joy as well as sustenance.

We've had good luck with handheld food—such as Onigiri (page 56) and Inari Sushi (page 55)—and my kids go wild for food they get to make themselves. A Temaki Party, where everybody constructs their own hand rolls, is a regular activity in our house (page 64). If your kids are a little bit older, the hot-pot meals in the Nabe section (pages 132 to 136) are great interactive food too.

At the end of the day, kids are going to like what they like. I don't believe anyone who tells me they have a recipe that will appeal to all children. The recipes in this section are the things that Chris and I have had success feeding our families. We've given you a lot of rice-based dishes and things that go on top of rice. Kids are programmed to like umami and starch, so our vegetable dishes mostly involve nestling vegetables in noodles and savory sauces. Hopefully some of these strategies will work for you too. Good luck out there.

Stuffed Tofu Pouches (Inari Sushi)

Makes 10 pieces

In Japan, inari sushi is usually convenience-store food, something you grab from the refrigerated section in Lawson's or Family Mart when you're in a rush. It's a perfectly portable snack—a little pouch of soy-simmered tofu encasing a clump of sushi rice—but when I buy it from the store, I usually find it's too cold or cloying and never especially delicious. (Don't get me wrong: The grab-and-go food in Japanese convenience stores would put many American restaurants to shame. I just think you can do better than that inari.)

I wish you could have seen the smile on my face when I took a bite of my first homemade inari. The rice was still warm and the tofu was sweet and savory—all the flavors were much more pronounced than in the cold premade versions. You should absolutely make inari—they're great for sticking in your kid's lunch and not at all difficult to pull off. I can eat two or three in a sitting and be satisfied for hours. (And if you're feeling especially lazy, you can buy preseasoned tofu pockets and skip straight to step 4.) Inari also takes extremely well to dressing up, with additions like wasabi, shiso, steamed carrots, or chopped spinach.

5 pieces unseasoned abura-age
   (fried tofu slices)
½ cup soy sauce
½ cup mirin
¼ cup sugar
1 tablespoon white sesame seeds
2½ cups Sushi Rice (page 26),
   still warm

1. Working with one piece at a time, lay the pieces of abura-age on a cutting board and cover with plastic wrap. Lightly run a rolling pin back and forth over the tofu 4 or 5 times. This makes it much easier to open the tofu into a "pocket" later. Cut each piece of abura-age crosswise in half.

2. Abura-age can be a little greasy when it comes out of the package. To remove some of the fat, place the abura-age in a colander in the sink, pour a few cups of boiling water over the top, and let sit for 10 minutes.

3. Combine the soy sauce, mirin, sugar, and 1½ cups water in a large saucepan over medium heat. Add the abura-age and bring to a simmer, then reduce the heat to low and cook for 10 minutes. Drain the abura-age.

4. Mix the sesame seeds into the rice with a spoon or rice paddle. Wet your hands and use your fingers to open each piece of abura-age into a pocket and stuff with ¼ cup rice. Once the rice is inside the pocket, form the abura-age into a little log and fold the excess tofu skin over to close it. Serve warm or pack them into your kid's bento box for lunch.

Rice Balls (Onigiri)

Makes as many as you like

When I first started entertaining the idea of opening a ramen shop in Japan, I kept stumbling over the question of how I could marry my sensibilities as a Western chef with the ramen-shop format. I wanted to offer things beyond ramen, but I wasn't sure what Japanese diners would accept and what would be anathema to them. I puzzled over this conundrum as I ate at ramen shop after ramen shop, doing research. (I know, life's tough.)

One day I came across a shop called Toride. The owner was really amiable, which wasn't always the case, and he had a handful of side dishes on offer, including a big fresh onigiri wrapped in seaweed, served with mentaiko (cod roe) mayo and pickles. It was very Japanese, but it opened my American mind to what else could be served in a ramen shop. Not to get too sentimental, but that experience instilled in me an extra level of comfort and confidence that made me feel like I could pull off a shop of my own. There's been a soft spot in my heart for onigiri ever since.

Much like Inari Sushi (page 55), onigiri make a perfect kids' snack or lunch. If your little ones appreciate the flavor of plain rice and nori, there's no need to get fancy. But for something more substantial, fill the onigiri with one of the suggestions that follow. Or, you can turn unfilled onigiri into Yaki Onigiri (Grilled Rice Balls, page 186)—one of the world's great bar snacks.

½ cup steamed rice (page 25) for each onigiri, warm but not hot

FOR SERVING
Nori sheets, sliced in half
Optional Fillings (recipes follow)

1. To make each onigiri, place a 1-foot square of plastic wrap on a cutting board and drop the warm rice into the center.

2. If you want to fill the onigiri, use your fingers or a spoon to flatten the rice into a layer about 1 inch thick. Place the filling in the center of the rice, then proceed, doing your best to keep the filling contained within the rice ball as you shape it. Gather the four corners of the plastic wrap together, lift up the rice, and twist the plastic together to force the rice together into a ball. Then use your hands to form the ball into a rough triangle, about 1 inch thick, twisting the plastic as necessary to compress the rice. This isn't an exact science. You're just using the plastic to help you form the rice. Remove the plastic and wrap the onigiri in a half-sheet of nori.

OPTIONAL FILLINGS
Each of these suggestions makes enough for one onigiri; scale up as desired.

BROILED SALMON (PAGE 113) OR MISO-GLAZED SALMON (PAGE 58):
Use a fork or your fingers to break the salmon into flakes. Use 1 tablespoon per onigiri.

TUNA MAYO: Mix together 1 tablespoon cooked, flaked tuna (the canned stuff is fine, but fresh is best) with 2 teaspoons Kewpie mayonnaise.

BONITO FLAKES WITH SOY SAUCE (OKARA): Stir together 2 tablespoons katsuobushi (bonito flakes) and 1½ teaspoons soy sauce.

PICKLED PLUM (UMEBOSHI): Remove the pit from 1 umeboshi (pickled plum) and chop it into a fine paste.

SEASONED GROUND CHICKEN (TORI SOBORO, PAGE 59): Use 1 tablespoon per onigiri.

RECIPE CONTINUES

Miso-Glazed Salmon (Sake Misozuke)

Serves 4 to 6 as a filling or topping

2 tablespoons miso, preferably
    white (shiro) or blended (awase)
2 teaspoons Kewpie mayonnaise
1½ teaspoons sake
½ teaspoon mirin
One 12-ounce skin-on salmon fillet

1. Whisk together the miso, Kewpie mayo, sake, and mirin in a small bowl. Coat the salmon fillet in the mixture and marinate for 20 minutes.

2. Heat the oven (or toaster oven) to 350°F.

3. Line a baking sheet with a wire rack or piece of foil, then place the salmon on top, skin side down.

Bake for 3 to 5 minutes, depending on the thickness of the fillet (3 minutes for a 1-inch-thick fillet; 5 minutes for a 2-inch piece).

4. Turn on the broiler and adjust the oven rack so that the fish sits about 6 inches below the heat source. Cook for 4 to 5 minutes more, until the fish is nicely browned and just cooked through.

Seasoned Ground Chicken (Tori Soboro)

Serves 4 as part of a larger meal

Tori soboro isn't really a complete dish unto itself. Think of it more like duct tape: not exactly thrilling on its own, but incredibly handy to have around. Paired with scrambled eggs, it's a classic topping for rice bowls and bento boxes. A lot of parents plate the chicken and egg in two symmetrical hemispheres with a line of sliced scallions down the middle, which the kids love. Sometimes I like to swap out scrambled egg in favor of a jiggly Hot-Spring Egg (Onsen Tamago, page 30). With or without egg, tori soboro makes for an easy filling option for a Temaki Party (page 64) or Onigiri (page 56)—roll a couple in the morning and toss them in your bag on the way out the door. At our house, we'll often make a big batch of Tori Soboro at the beginning of the week, and use it in different ways over the next couple days.

One pro tip: If you happen to have some Tare (Seasoning Sauce, page 97) on hand, you can simply sauté the ground chicken in vegetable oil, then season with ⅓ cup tare mixed with 2 tablespoons water.

2 tablespoons soy sauce

1 tablespoon plus 1 teaspoon sake

1 tablespoon plus 1 teaspoon mirin

1 teaspoon sugar

1 tablespoon minced ginger

1 tablespoon vegetable oil

1 pound ground chicken

FOR SERVING

Steamed rice (page 25)

Hot-Spring Eggs (Onsen Tamago, page 30) or scrambled eggs

Slivered scallion greens

1. Combine the soy sauce, sake, mirin, sugar, and ginger with 2 tablespoons water in a bowl and whisk to dissolve the sugar. Set aside.

2. Heat a large skillet over high heat, then coat with the vegetable oil. Once the oil is hot, add the ground chicken and use a spoon or spatula to break up any clumps. Add the sauce mixture and simmer for 3 to 5 minutes, stirring constantly, until most of the sauce has evaporated or been absorbed by the chicken. Serve over warm rice, with the eggs on top or to the side of the chicken. Garnish with scallion greens.

Teriyaki 12.0

Makes 1 cup

In general, the Orkins probably eat less meat than your average American family. Living in Tokyo, we never sat down to a dinner where each of the five of us got his or her own big-ass piece of steak. Much more common was sharing one steak—grilled and sliced and enjoyed with an assortment of other dishes. And more often than not, it would be drizzled with teriyaki sauce.

Teriyaki is the embodiment of the sweet-soy flavor that so many people associate with Japanese food. You might think it's a little hackneyed, but let's be honest: Teriyaki rules. It's a lifesaver for weekday dinners, and you can also employ it for more elaborate projects like slow-cooked ribs. Believe me when I tell you I've been through a ton of teriyaki recipes over the years. This one's my favorite. It requires just five easy-to-remember ingredients (bottled oyster sauce is the only wild card, and it's a great addition), and then you're in teriyaki town.

¼ **cup sake**

¼ **cup mirin**

¼ **cup soy sauce**

¼ **cup oyster sauce**

1 **tablespoon sugar**

Whisk together all the ingredients in a bowl until the sugar is dissolved. You're good to go. Store in the fridge for up to a couple weeks.

FOR BEEF OR PORK

Panfry or grill a piece of meat (hanger, bavette, skirt, or boneless rib-eye steaks all work well, as do boneless pork chops and pork tenderloin) to medium-rare or your desired doneness. Allow to rest for a few minutes, then cut against the grain into ½-inch-thick slices and arrange on a platter. Meanwhile, bring the teriyaki sauce to a simmer in a skillet over medium heat and cook until reduced to a syrupy consistency, 3 to 4 minutes. Pour over the sliced meat and serve with warm rice.

FOR CHICKEN

Dust 4 or 5 boneless, skinless chicken thighs with all-purpose flour. Brown the chicken on both sides in a well-oiled nonstick pan over medium heat. Once the chicken is browned, add the teriyaki sauce, bring to a simmer, and cook until reduced to a syrupy consistency, 3 to 4 minutes, flipping the chicken pieces to coat them. Serve over warm rice.

FOR FISH

Place a nonstick or well-seasoned carbon steel skillet over medium heat and coat with oil, then carefully lay a large fillet of firm fish (salmon, halibut, yellowtail, or black cod) in the pan. Brown the fish on both sides, then add the teriyaki sauce, bring to a simmer, and cook until reduced to a syrupy consistency, 3 to 4 minutes, flipping the fish to coat it. Serve over warm rice.

FOR PORK RIBS

Slice a rack of ribs into 3-rib segments and add to a large zip-top plastic bag. Add the teriyaki sauce and massage it into the meat. Seal the bag, forcing out as much air as you can, and marinate overnight in the fridge. The next day, grill the ribs slowly over low heat until tender, glazing with the marinade remaining in the bag. Finish over high heat to get a nice crust on the ribs.

Stir-Fried Udon (Yaki Udon)

Serves 4

In my experience, if you tangle vegetables in a mess of fried noodles, your kids will be much more likely to eat them. To that end, yaki udon is a family-friendly stir-fry that's heavy on plants and fungi.

There are a couple shortcuts I lean on to make this recipe manageable on a busy Monday night. I'm sure there will be some purists who object to my methods, but I'm also fairly confident that those people don't have three kids running amok in their house. First: frozen udon. You'll find frozen blocks of cooked udon noodles in the freezer section of most Asian markets. Using frozen noodles means you don't have to boil a pot of water to cook dried noodles. Second: the microwave. Nuking some of the vegetables for a few minutes will cut down your cooking time dramatically, and you honestly won't notice a difference in taste.

NOODLES AND VEGETABLES

1 pound frozen udon

½ small head cabbage, cut into 2-inch squares

1 large carrot, peeled and cut into matchsticks

3 ounces shimeji (beech) or oyster mushrooms

SAUCE

½ cup soy sauce

2 tablespoons sake

2 tablespoons mirin

2 tablespoons oyster sauce

8 ounces thinly sliced skinless pork belly (see Thinly Sliced Meat, page 129) or uncured bacon, cut into 1-inch pieces

1 tablespoon minced garlic

4 scallions, sliced lengthwise in half and cut into 1-inch lengths

1 red bell pepper, cored, seeded, and cut into matchsticks

2 teaspoons toasted sesame oil

½ cup tightly packed katsuobushi (bonito flakes)

1. **FOR THE NOODLES:** Place the udon in a colander and run under hot water to defrost the noodles. Alternatively, put them in a bowl and microwave for 1 minute. Set aside while you prep the vegetables.

2. **FOR THE VEGETABLES:** Place the cabbage and carrot in a microwave-safe container and zap them for 2 minutes. If you've managed to locate some shimejis, cut off the bottoms and separate the mushrooms. If you're using oyster mushrooms, give them a quick rinse and slice them into ½-inch-wide strips.

3. **FOR THE SAUCE:** Stir all the ingredients together in a bowl; set aside.

4. Set a large nonstick skillet over medium-high heat and add the pork belly or bacon. Sauté until the meat is mostly cooked through, 3 to 4 minutes.

5. Add the garlic and cook until fragrant, about 30 seconds. Add the scallions and bell pepper and cook until slightly softened, about 2 minutes. Follow with the mushrooms and cook for 2 minutes. Finally, add the microwave-softened cabbage and carrots and cook until you start to see some browning along the edges of the vegetables, 3 to 4 minutes more. Scoop the pork and vegetables into a bowl and set aside. Give the pan a quick wipe with a paper towel and return it to the stove.

6. Turn the heat up to high and coat the pan with the sesame oil. Add the udon and sauté until you begin to see some crisp edges on the noodles, about 2 minutes. Add the pork and vegetables and toss to combine. Add the sauce and toss to coat. Leave the pan on the heat for another minute to thicken the sauce, then fold in the katsuobushi and serve.

Okinawan Stir-Fry (Chanpuru)

Serves 4

This is the classic dish of Okinawa, a stir-fry that can include anything from Spam to fish to bacon but almost always has tofu and bitter melon. I like bitter melon, but its astringency is an acquired taste and I know it's a nonstarter for a lot of people (especially children), so I've omitted it in this version. By all means, if you love it, add some: Split a melon in half, scrape out the seeds, and cut it into thin half-moons. That's the nice thing about chanpuru—it can be anything you want. At my house, as long as we have tofu and fatty pork on hand (and we usually do), we can have chanpuru, made with whatever vegetables are sitting in the crisper drawer.

8 ounces thinly sliced skinless pork belly (see Thinly Sliced Meat, page 129) or uncured bacon, cut into 1-inch pieces

½ large onion, sliced thin

10 button mushrooms, trimmed and sliced thin

1 zucchini, halved lengthwise and sliced thin

2 cups bean sprouts, rinsed

One 14-ounce package firm tofu, drained and cut into 1-inch cubes

2 tablespoons soy sauce

2 teaspoons toasted sesame oil

1½ teaspoons kosher salt

2 cups firmly packed katsuobushi (bonito flakes)

FOR SERVING
Steamed rice (page 25)

1. Place the pork belly or bacon in a large skillet set over high heat and cook until a good bit of the fat has rendered, about 4 minutes.

2. Add the onion to the pan and cook for 3 to 4 minutes, stirring constantly, until softened. Toss in the mushrooms and zucchini and cook for 3 minutes. Add the sprouts, tofu, soy sauce, sesame oil, and salt, toss to combine everything thoroughly—don't worry if the tofu breaks apart—and cook until the sprouts are wilted but still crunchy, about 2 minutes.

3. Remove from the heat and fold in the katsuobushi. Serve with rice.

Temaki Party

Serves 6

Temaki sushi (hand rolls) are hugely popular with my kids, partly because they all love sushi, but also because it allows them to eat however they like. At least once every couple months, we'll have a temaki party. Everyone gets a bowl of rice and a stack of nori, and we all go to town making our own rolls filled with ingredients arranged in the center of the table. This works equally well as a dinner party for adults. I'd almost never consider making sushi for more than one or two people at home—it's way too much work—but a temaki party frees you up to chat and entertain guests while everyone's busy assembling their own hand rolls.

Your work consists entirely of shopping, prep, and setting the table. Granted, a temaki party is easier to pull off in a country like Japan where you can find sushi-grade fish in practically any market, but it's totally possible in the States if you have access to a Japanese market or a reputable place to buy fresh fish. You can ask the fishmongers at nicer grocery stores to order fish for you if they don't always have everything you want in stock. And if your local fish selection is really slim, not to worry: You can always supplement with cooked items like Kimchi Pork Belly (Buta Kimchi, page 74) and Miso-Glazed Salmon (Sake Misozuke, page 58), plus vegetables like avocado, cucumber, and shiso leaves.

There is no set path to success here—it's a truly forgiving way of hosting a dinner party. Nevertheless, here's a rundown of the three basic components of a temaki party—the rice, the nori, and the fillings—along with some guidelines for assembly.

RICE

As I noted earlier, properly cooked and seasoned rice is an under-appreciated component of sushi in the States. That being said, on most nights that we host a temaki party, I go the easy route and serve unseasoned short-grain rice that's been cooked in a rice cooker, and it works great. Two cups of raw rice should make plenty for six people. But if you want to make proper sushi rice, see page 26.

NORI

It's honestly very difficult to tell the difference between various brands of nori from the packages. Eventually you'll find a kind you like, but it may take some trial and error to land on one that's aromatic and crisp, rather than lifeless and papery. If your options are limited, just buy what you can get—even packages of presliced, seasoned seaweed squares will be fine.

If you're working with whole sheets of nori, cut each piece into quarters and give each person about 10 squares to start. If you're so inclined, you can toast each sheet of nori before slicing by waving it over an open flame for 10 to 15 seconds. Don't get too close or linger too long over the flame, or the nori will shrivel and burn. But don't be too shy either, or the seaweed won't pick up any toasty flavor.

FILLINGS

Provide your guests with a nice mix of cooked and raw protein, plus plenty of fresh herbs and veggies. It doesn't take much to fill a temaki, but you want to have enough of each filling so that everyone can have a taste. As for what to buy, the world is your oyster. Pick whatever you and your family like. As a guideline, here's what I would set out for six people:

SEAFOOD: You'll want ¼ to ½ pound each of four or five different fish. Tuna is the standard choice. Any sushi-grade tuna will

RECIPE CONTINUES

do, but let's all please steer clear of endangered bluefin. Otherwise I like a combination of sea bass (suzuki), yellowtail (hamachi), chopped tuna mixed with Japanese scallions (negitoro), scallops (hotate), fluke (hirame), and ikura (cured salmon roe). Chris and I both love oily fish like mackerel (saba) and sardine (iwashi), but choose whatever you like.

Depending on where you buy your fish, you may need to slice it yourself. (If you buy it from a Japanese market or specialty fish shop, it may come presliced.) Do your best to cut it into ¼-inch-thick slices on the bias, across the grain of the fish. Take your time and use a long, sharp knife. If you're not confident in your slicing skills, just cut the fish into cubes. No one's judging.

COOKED ITEMS: Choose one or two of the following and serve warm or at room temperature.

Kimchi Pork Belly (Buta Kimchi, page 74)
Miso-Glazed Salmon (Sake Misozuke, page 58)
Seasoned Ground Chicken (Tori Soboro, page 59)

VEGETABLES AND HERBS:
1 or 2 avocados, halved, pitted, peeled, and sliced thin
½ cucumber (Japanese, Persian, or English), seeded and cut into batons
About 20 shiso leaves
2 whole myoga (Japanese ginger), cut into long, thin slices (optional)

CONDIMENTS: Here's your chance to bust out the nice shoyu. Don't sully your high-quality fish with crappy soy sauce; find an artisanal brand you like. As for wasabi, if you have access to fresh roots, that's fantastic. If not, the squeezable paste that comes in a tube will be fine.

ASSEMBLY

Provide each of your guests with a bowl of rice, a stack of nori, and a little ramekin of soy sauce. Set the bowls and plates of fillings in the middle of the table for everyone to share. There's no wrong way to make temaki, but here's the gist of it: Hold a square of nori in one hand and spread a small scoop of rice on top. Smear a little wasabi on the rice, then lay the fillings in a line down the center. Try not to pack the roll so full that fish and rice will spill out the sides. Roll it up like a taco, give it a light dip in soy sauce, and eat.

Open to Anything

A Long Tradition of Mixing

When I was fifteen, my friend got me a job washing dishes at the Japanese restaurant where he worked on Long Island. I didn't know anything about Japan or Japanese culture beyond what I'd seen in movies, but it seemed like a good way to make a buck. At work, when the Japanese cooks spoke to one another, all I heard was unintelligible chatter. But when they addressed me, they were unfailingly kind. The food they were serving was completely foreign to me, but they always shared, and I found it delicious and intriguing.

More important, for the first time in my life, I felt a connection to something. I didn't know what exactly—working in a restaurant, maybe, or Japanese food, or Japanese people. I felt it in my gut, and I needed more. I left that job when I was sixteen. Except for the occasional sushi meal, I didn't really see much of Japanese food or culture for a few years, but that feeling never went away. I studied Japanese in college, and in the subsequent three decades, I've been edging closer and closer to touching the source.

I realize I'll never be a real Japanese person—I'm not delusional. There are parts of being born in Japan and being ethnically Japanese that I'm not going to pretend I'll ever grasp. But I've learned over time to enjoy being Jewish, American, and Japanese all at the same time. In truth, my success as a ramen chef in Japan came down to the fact that I'm not Japanese, I'm a gaijin. My soup was unique and special because I built it using skills and ingredients from different worlds. Ironically, my readiness to meld ideas from different worlds was the most Japanese thing I could do.

Japan has an unfair reputation for being closed off, resistant to outside influence. If you walk into an unfamiliar restaurant in Tokyo, you might be met with blank stares that you'll take as a sign that the owners don't want you there. But the experience I've had living and working in Tokyo for decades is much more nuanced. If I'd felt that Japanese people were universally hostile to outsiders, I wouldn't have stayed so long.

Beneath the surface, you'll find that Japanese food—like all great cuisines—is a blend of different traditions and ingredients from around the world. Some of those fusions were violent and unpredictable—products of war and conquest—but others have been organic and coordinated. In other words, many of the dishes we know today as Japanese can be traced to other places and times. (The same can be said for American food.) This chapter is a celebration of such cultural collisions.

Yoshoku (Western Cooking)

Japanese people refer to food with origins outside of Japan as *yoshoku,* or "Western cooking." These include dishes you might have eaten dozens of times in restaurants in the States—croquettes and curry and fried shrimp. But there are others in this category that Americans are less familiar with, like cream stew, which has French roots, and spaghetti Napolitan—the Japanese take on tomato-sauced pasta.

When I first moved to Tokyo, a lot of the fancy restaurants were yoshoku places. The chefs would all be wearing toques and neckerchiefs, like Iron

Top left: A prototypical Japanese egg sandwich—fluffy, squishy, perfect.
Top right: Bagels from my friend's shop Kepo Bagels.
Bottom right: A plate of spaghetti Napolitan at Seiyoken in Ueno.
Bottom left: Japanese curry is a perfect example of yoshoku food.

Chef Sakai, and the service would be formal French, but the food would be Japanese-inflected, with courses like omurice (an omelet draped over rice and covered in ketchup) and hayashi rice (rich beef stew over rice).

These days yoshoku food is much more integrated into the broader culinary culture. Chris once asked me if I ever felt a connection to my Western upbringing through yoshoku food. The truth is, as an outsider in Japan, it can be hard to see the lines. Sometimes I'll be raving about something I ate in Japan, and my wife will point out that it actually originated in Portugal. But perhaps the surest sign that yoshoku has been synthesized fully into the Japanese canon is the nostalgia Japanese diners feel for it. It's comfort food to them, the same way that hamburgers and pizza (also foods imported from elsewhere) soothe American souls.

Ivan Ramen Recipes

Being a lifelong gaijin has taught me the value of an outsider's perspective. A curious, humble outsider is perceptive, empathetic, and open to new ways of doing things. As I mentioned above, being an outsider is what made my ramen special. But when I first set out to open a ramen shop, I found myself paralyzed with anxiety about messing with Japanese food. I didn't know how far I could push things, and I feared it might be disrespectful to futz around too much with the status quo.

As odd as it sounds, the first time I cooked a decent bowl of ramen was at a Passover dinner in Tokyo. I was at home, cooking for friends, so I felt comfortable fucking with both my own traditions and those of my diners. Combining what I knew about Jewish chicken soup with what I loved about Japanese ramen, I ended up with a dish where it all clicked beautifully into place. It was delicious, and nobody was offended, leaving me more confident that maybe Ivan Ramen would work.

I continue to have great reverence and love for Japanese traditions, but years of study have showed me that the lines between what is and isn't Japanese are less clear than I once thought. Without tooting my own horn too hard, I think that this realization has led me to create some pretty great, unexpected dishes, which I'll share in this chapter.

My friend Yamauchi-san, who came to me for advice once she decided to switch careers and open a bagel shop in Tokyo. I may have given her a nudge in the right direction, but she really took the concept and made it her own.

Kimchi Pork Belly (Buta Kimchi)

Serves 4

The Japanese have a remarkable ability to adopt dishes and foods from other places. Take, for instance, that most Korean of ingredients, kimchi. You'll find kimchi in practically every grocery store in Japan, as well as on the menus of numerous izakayas. I adore this aspect of Japanese dining culture. The only true requirement for something to be considered Japanese is for Japanese people to love it.

This is a recipe for a super-simple sauté of kimchi, pork belly, garlic chives, and crunchy bean sprouts. Japanese kimchi tends to be a little sweeter than its Korean counterpart, but if you can only find the spicy stuff, and you have family members who are timid about spice, add a little extra sugar to the sauce to balance the heat. On the other hand, if you like things spicy, feel free to add some red pepper flakes to the mix.

¼ cup soy sauce

2 tablespoons mirin

2 tablespoons sake

2 tablespoons oyster sauce

2 tablespoons sugar

1 teaspoon toasted sesame oil

12 ounces thinly sliced skinless pork belly (see Thinly Sliced Meat, page 129) or uncured bacon, cut into 1-inch pieces

4 ounces garlic chives (nira), sliced into 1-inch lengths (about 2 cups)

8 ounces kimchi, chopped into 1-inch pieces (about 1¼ cups)

2 cups (about 9 ounces) bean sprouts

FOR SERVING
Steamed rice (page 25)

1. Whisk together the soy sauce, mirin, sake, oyster sauce, and sugar in a bowl and set aside.

2. Heat a large skillet or wok over high heat, then coat with the sesame oil. Add the pork belly and cook for 3 to 4 minutes, stirring regularly, until most of the fat has rendered and the meat is cooked through.

3. Add the chives and cook until wilted, about 30 seconds. Stir in the kimchi and sauce mixture and bring to a simmer. Fold in the bean sprouts and cook for 2 to 3 more minutes, until the sauce has thickened slightly and the sprouts are wilted but still crunchy. Serve with steamed rice.

Spaghetti Napolitan

Serves 2

To any Italians reading this: Please avert your eyes.

Everyone else, we're going to make spaghetti with ketchup sauce. On second thought, Italian friends, maybe you should read this. I know that spaghetti with ketchup sounds blasphemous, but consider that Italian food is actually an amalgamation of dozens of cultural influences, from Chinese noodles to New World tomatoes. As cultures met and ingredients were exchanged over the course of hundreds of years, a cuisine emerged. And it's not a static thing. Spaghetti Napolitan is simply another step in that same tradition. It's still spaghetti and its roots are Italian, but it's taken on a completely new life in Japan, where office workers eat huge plates of the stuff for lunch, somehow avoiding stains on their collared white shirts, then smoke a cigarette and head back to their jobs. To appreciate spaghetti Napolitan is to understand the Japanese working stiff.

Maybe you still object to the idea of ketchup as pasta sauce. You shouldn't. Cooking the ketchup gives it more depth and tempers the sweetness, and the bacon lends its smokiness. Honestly, you'll have a hard time remembering that you're eating ketchup.

Kosher salt

5 strips bacon, sliced into 1-inch pieces

½ large onion, sliced thin

1 small red bell pepper, cored, seeded, and sliced thin

1 tablespoon minced garlic

6 white button mushrooms, trimmed and sliced ⅛ inch thick

¾ cup ketchup

8 ounces dried spaghetti

1 tablespoon unsalted butter

FOR SERVING

Tabasco sauce

Grated Parmesan (in Tokyo it's always the stuff from the green Kraft can)

1. Bring a large pot of salted water to a boil. Meanwhile, start the sauce: Add the bacon to a large skillet and cook over medium-low heat until it's rendered its fat and is just shy of crisp, about 6 minutes. Transfer the bacon to a paper towel with a slotted spoon and discard all but about ¼ cup of the rendered fat in the pan.

2. Return the pan to the stove and turn the heat up to medium. Cook the onion in the bacon fat, stirring, until softened and beginning to turn color, about 5 minutes. Add the bell pepper, garlic, and mushrooms and cook until all of the vegetables are softened but not falling apart, another 6 minutes or so.

3. Stir in the ketchup and cook until it begins to lose some of its gloss, about 3 minutes. Remove the sauce from the heat and set aside.

4. Cook the pasta according to the package directions until al dente. Add a few big spoonfuls of pasta water to the sauce and drain the pasta. Return the sauce to medium-high heat and add the pasta, bacon, and butter. Mix thoroughly with tongs or chopsticks to ensure that all the noodles are coated, then cook for a couple minutes to allow them to soak up the sauce. Portion into bowls and serve with Tabasco sauce and Parmesan.

Mentaiko Spaghetti

Serves 2

Mentaiko spaghetti is a perfect example of yoshoku food. You take one look at it and you immediately know it's Japanese even though you're staring at a bowl of Italian pasta. The noodles are coated in cream and butter and fish roe, with a big fistful of shredded shiso leaves and nori piled on top. You'll find it at pasta restaurants throughout Japan, with a tiny salad and a glass of iced coffee on the side.

You're probably not going to come across mentaiko spaghetti in many American restaurants, but the good news is that you can make it at home without breaking a sweat. Finding mentaiko is the only obstacle. Mentaiko is cod or pollock roe that has been marinated in togarashi. The eggs are tiny and come bundled in their natural sacs, which you have to split open and scrape the roe from. (Tarako, cured but not chili-spiced roe, is a fine substitute.) Unfortunately, if you don't have a Japanese or Korean market within reach, you probably won't find mentaiko or tarako. They do sell packets of premade mentaiko pasta sauce online that aren't half bad, if you're desperate.

I wouldn't try to make this in a bigger batch than what's suggested here, or things will start to clump and become unmanageable. If you're serving a large group, work two servings at a time.

Kosher salt

8 ounces dried spaghetti

3 tablespoons unsalted butter, cut into small cubes, at room temp

2 tablespoons heavy cream

1 teaspoon soy sauce

4 sacs mentaiko (cod or pollock roe; 3 to 4 ounces total), split open and roe gently scraped out

½ cup shredded nori (or 1 sheet nori, toasted over a flame and cut into matchsticks)

8 shiso leaves, large leaves cut into ribbons

1. This will go pretty quickly, so make sure you have all your ingredients prepped and measured before you start cooking. Once you're organized, bring a large pot of water to a boil and season liberally with salt—the water should taste like the ocean. Add the spaghetti and cook according to the package directions until al dente.

2. Drain the pasta in a colander and give it a good shake to shed as much water as possible. Add the pasta to a large glass or ceramic bowl, along with the butter, and stir with tongs or chopsticks until the butter is mostly melted. Add the cream, soy sauce, and ½ teaspoon salt and toss and stir, then gently mix in the mentaiko until evenly distributed throughout the pasta. Divide the pasta among two bowls, top with piles of the nori and shiso, and serve immediately.

Stuffed Cabbage (Roru Kyabetsu)

Serves 4 to 6

What's this stuffed cabbage recipe doing in a Japanese cookbook? Is it, like, stuffed with fish and cherry blossoms? Nope. It's stuffed cabbage more or less the way your Polish grandmother made it.

Yoshoku food can be a funny thing. Often these "Western-style" dishes have evolved considerably from their forebears into something that looks and feels distinctly Japanese. Other times, as with this stuffed cabbage, there's little discernible change from the original, yet Japanese diners embrace it wholeheartedly as Japanese. Using dashi as the braising liquid gives the cabbage a nice hit of smoke and umami, but otherwise it's basically the same dish it was when it first arrived in Japan from Europe.

1 large head green cabbage
1½ pounds ground beef (fattier is better)
1 large egg, beaten
½ onion, finely chopped
½ cup panko
2 tablespoons ketchup
1 tablespoon soy sauce
2 teaspoons kosher salt
4 cups Dashi (page 28)
One 28-ounce can crushed tomatoes

1. Fill a large pot halfway with water and bring it to a boil. Carefully cut the core out of the cabbage (don't worry about removing all of it) and loosen the outer leaves from the base. Stick a fork into the hole where the core used to be and lower the whole head into the boiling water. Gently roll the head back and forth to submerge all of the outer leaves, then use another fork to peel them off into the water as they loosen. You're looking to harvest 7 or 8 intact large leaves. Once you have enough, lower the heat, remove the head, and let the separated leaves simmer for 8 more minutes. Meanwhile, prepare an ice bath in a large bowl. Drain the cooked cabbage leaves in a colander, then plunge them into the ice bath to cool. Drain and pat dry. Reserve the rest of the cabbage for another use.

2. Combine the ground beef, egg, onion, panko, ketchup, soy sauce, and salt in a bowl and mix with your hands until everything is blended, but don't overwork it.

3. Lay a cabbage leaf on a work surface and spoon about ½ cup of the beef mixture into the center of the leaf. Fold the sides of the leaf over, then roll it up from the bottom to form a cylinder. Use a couple toothpicks to secure the roll. Repeat with the remaining leaves and filling.

4. Combine the dashi and crushed tomatoes in a Dutch oven or other large heavy-bottomed pot and set over medium heat. Nestle the cabbage rolls in the liquid. Don't worry if you can't get all of them submerged—you can move them around as they cook. Bring the liquid to a simmer, then drop the heat to low and cook until the cabbage is completely tender and the meat is cooked through, about 1 hour.

5. Serve one or two cabbage rolls per plate (remember to remove the toothpicks), and top them with a big spoonful of smoky tomato sauce.

Stuffed Peppers
(Piiman no Nikuzume)

Serves 4

Here's another yoshoku dish that doesn't feel very much changed from its Western origins. Stuffing whole peppers with a delicious filling is a concept that is part of many different culinary traditions, from Mexico to Macedonia. The Japanese version bears a close resemblance to what you'll find on suburban tables all over America except that bell peppers in Japan are a little smaller and thinner skinned (and much more expensive).

I have a special affection for this recipe because it's one of the dishes in my wife's tightly curated repertoire. As a chef, I end up with a lot of the responsibility of cooking at home, but my wife will occasionally take the reins, and I love it when she does. I'm a sucker for anything with ketchup and Bull-Dog sauce, but I think Mari's stuffed peppers stand up to anyone's in New York or Tokyo.

1 pound ground beef (fatty is better)

1 large egg, beaten

½ medium onion, finely chopped

2 tablespoons ketchup

1 cup panko

½ teaspoon kosher salt

2 large green bell peppers, halved lengthwise and seeded

FOR SERVING

Ketchup

Bull-Dog tonkatsu sauce

1. Heat the oven to 350°F. (I use my toaster oven, which works great.) Line a baking sheet with foil.

2. Combine the beef, egg, onion, ketchup, panko, and salt in a bowl and mix thoroughly. Stuff the mixture into the peppers. There should be enough to fill each half-pepper generously, with some of the mixture brimming over the top by about ½ inch.

3. Arrange the peppers on the baking sheet and bake until they have softened and the meat is cooked through, about 45 minutes. Meanwhile, stir together a 50:50 blend of ketchup and Bull-Dog sauce. Top the cooked peppers with a few generous spoonfuls of sauce and serve.

Pork Curry from the Box

Serves 4

Although curry originated in India, it has since spread widely and unstoppably. It has grown and evolved wherever it landed, including Japan, where it tends to be a little sweeter and fruitier than other curries.

If you've ever had Japanese curry, whether in a restaurant or a home, it was most likely made from a store-bought box of roux blocks that dissolve in liquid to make a perfectly thickened, shiny sauce. Boxed Japanese curry is magnificent, and I will go to the mat with anyone who argues otherwise. The Japanese are masters of packaged food. But obviously you didn't buy this book to learn how to follow the directions on the back of a box, so I'm going to let you in on a couple of boxed-curry hacks we use in the Orkin household.

First we up the ante by braising a pork shoulder and using the meat and braising liquid as the base for the curry. Second, because we eat curry so often, I usually braise way more pork shoulder than I need, then portion the meat and liquid into three batches and freeze the extras. That way, whenever we want curry, all I have to do is thaw a batch of braised pork, add some water and vegetables, and toss in the boxed mix.

As for what kind of curry to buy, all of the brands (Golden, Java, Vermont, etc.) are fine, but I stick to the mild versions for the kids. Sometimes we'll slip a little milk and honey into the curry to make it even sweeter and more appealing to them. (If you can't find boxed curry or don't want to use it, see the recipe for Pork Curry from Scratch, page 86.)

VEGETABLES

1 tablespoon vegetable oil

2 medium carrots, peeled and cut into 1-inch pieces

1 large russet potato or Japanese sweet potato, cut into large chunks

1 onion, cut into large chunks

MEAT AND CURRY

⅓ recipe Braised Pork (opposite), with the braising liquid, thawed if frozen

One 8-ounce box Japanese curry blocks (see headnote)

½ cup whole milk (optional)

2 tablespoons honey (optional)

FOR SERVING

Steamed rice (page 25)

Fukujin pickles or pickled sushi ginger

1. Heat a Dutch oven or other large heavy-bottomed pot over medium-high heat, then coat with the vegetable oil. Add the carrots and potato and cook for 4 minutes, stirring regularly. Add the onion and cook for 2 more minutes to remove some of the rawness.

2. Use a slotted spoon to scoop the pork chunks into the pot. Now measure how much braising liquid you have and add enough water to total 5 cups of liquid, then add to the pot. Bring to a simmer, lower the heat to medium, and cook until the carrots and potato are nearly tender, 3 to 5 minutes.

3. Break up the curry blocks and stir them into the pot. (It'll take some diligence to make sure they're all completely dissolved.) If you like your curry a little richer/sweeter, stir in the milk and honey. Simmer for 5 minutes, then serve over steamed rice with little piles of pickles on the side.

Braised Pork

Makes enough for 3 batches
of curry

One 5-pound boneless pork
    shoulder, cut into 2-inch chunks
1 tablespoon plus 1 teaspoon
    kosher salt
1½ teaspoons freshly ground black
    pepper
2 tablespoons vegetable oil
8 cups Dashi (page 28), chicken
    stock, water, or a combination

1. Preheat the oven to 350°F.

2. Season the pork with the salt
and pepper. Heat a Dutch oven or
other large heavy-bottomed pot
over medium-high heat, then coat
with the vegetable oil. Working in
batches, sear the pork pieces on all
sides. Don't crowd the pot, or you'll
end up steaming rather than searing
the meat. All told, you should spend
a good 15 minutes or so, making
sure all of the meat gets some good
color and removing the pieces to a
bowl or plate as they brown. Once

all the meat is browned, pour off
the fat and return the meat to the
pot. Add the dashi, chicken stock,
or water and bring to a simmer,
then cover the pot and slide it in the
oven. Cook for about 2 hours, or
until the meat is fork-tender.

3. Reserve one-third of the meat
and broth for your first batch of
curry. Let the rest of the pork and
broth cool to room temperature
before portioning it into two plastic containers and freezing it for
future curry dinners.

Pork Curry from Scratch

Serves 4 to 6

To be completely honest, I rarely make curry from scratch. The packaged roux bricks are so convenient and so good, they're hard to beat, especially if you do it my way (see page 43). However, there's something undeniably gratifying about curry made without the assistance of industrial food science. Homemade curry doesn't have the supernatural shininess or smooth consistency of the sauce from the boxed stuff, but you can customize the seasoning with your choice of curry powder, whether it's Japanese, Indian, Chinese, or a spice mix of your own devising.

This recipe still comes together pretty quickly, even without those curry bricks. The secret is that you're still not totally free of packaged food: I count on Bull-Dog tonkatsu sauce and ketchup to pull some of the flavor weight.

2 tablespoons vegetable oil

1¼ pounds boneless pork shoulder or boneless country-style ribs, cut into 1-inch cubes

2 large onions, roughly chopped

2 tablespoons minced ginger

2 tablespoons minced garlic

1 large russet potato, peeled and cut into large chunks

1 large carrot, peeled and cut into 1-inch chunks

1 tablespoon kosher salt

3 tablespoons unsalted butter

2 tablespoons all-purpose flour

¼ cup curry powder (I like S&B brand)

4 cups chicken stock, Dashi (page 28), or water

3 tablespoons ketchup

3 tablespoons Bull-Dog tonkatsu sauce

Soy sauce

FOR SERVING

Steamed rice (page 25)

Fukujin pickles or pickled sushi ginger

1. Heat a Dutch oven or other large heavy-bottomed pot over medium heat, then coat with 1 tablespoon of the vegetable oil. Working in batches if necessary, brown the pork on all sides. Take a good 10 to 15 minutes to render the fat and achieve some nice browning. As the pieces are browned, transfer them to a bowl or plate.

2. Pour off all but 1 tablespoon of the fat from the pot. Add the onions and cook until they're slightly softened and beginning to brown around the edges, about 5 minutes. Stir in the ginger and garlic and cook until fragrant, about 2 minutes more. Stir in the potato and carrot, season with the salt, and cook for 4 minutes, stirring regularly.

3. Return the meat and any accumulated juices to the pan. Add the remaining 1 tablespoon oil and the butter to the pot and let the butter melt. Mix the flour and curry powder together, then sprinkle evenly over the vegetables and meat. Stir to distribute the flour-curry mix, pour in the stock or water, and stir again to combine. Bring to a simmer, then drop the heat to low and stir in the ketchup and Bull-Dog sauce. Cook until the meat and vegetables are tender, 30 to 40 minutes, stirring occasionally to prevent scorching.

4. Season the curry to taste with soy sauce and serve over steamed rice with a side of pickles.

Chicken Cream Stew (Kurimu Shichu)

Serves 4

Unlike curry rice or tonkatsu or other cross-cultural specimens, cream stew isn't something you're likely to come across in a Japanese-American restaurant, but you'll find it at any yoshoku (Western-style) place in Japan. In fact, there are restaurants in Tokyo that are wholly devoted to cream stew. They'll serve something like fifty different varieties of *doria*—casseroles of rice topped with cream stew and cheese that are browned under a broiler. My wife loves it.

Not many people make cream stew from scratch these days. Boxes of cream stew mix sit right next to the packaged curry sauce blocks in the grocery stores in Japan. They're less available in the States, but making cream stew without the premade stuff is easy enough. The only secret is to keep the heat low and watch the color of the flour—you want a cream stew that's velvety and white, not brown.

1 large boneless, skinless chicken breast (about 1 pound), cut into 1-inch chunks

1½ teaspoons kosher salt

1 tablespoon vegetable oil

2 onions, cut into medium dice

1 large carrot, peeled and cut into ½-inch-thick slices

2 Yukon Gold potatoes, peeled and cut into medium dice

5 tablespoons unsalted butter, cut into rough cubes

¼ cup plus 1 tablespoon all-purpose flour

3 cups whole milk

1 tablespoon white (shiro) miso

FOR SERVING
Steamed rice (page 25)
Pickled sushi ginger

1. Season the chicken with the salt. Set aside while you cook the vegetables.

2. Heat a Dutch oven or other large heavy-bottomed pot over medium-low heat, then coat with the vegetable oil. Add the onions and sauté until translucent, about 5 minutes. Add the carrot and potatoes and cook for another 3 minutes, stirring occasionally.

3. Add the chicken to the pot and cook until the pieces have mostly turned white, about 3 minutes. Add the butter and stir to melt it. Once the butter's melted, sprinkle the flour evenly over the meat and vegetables, stir to incorporate, and cook, stirring constantly, for 1½ minutes. You want to remove some of the raw flavor from the flour, but you're not trying to brown it, and you definitely don't want to burn it.

4. Gradually add the milk and allow it to come to a simmer, stirring. Add the miso to a small bowl and ladle in some of the sauce from the pot, whisking until smooth, then stir the mixture into the stew. The miso takes a little work to dissolve—doing it this way prevents lumps from slipping past you.

5. Cover the pot and turn down the heat as low as it will go. Simmer gently, stirring every couple minutes, for 10 to 15 minutes, until the potatoes and carrot are perfectly tender. Serve over steamed rice, with plenty of pickled ginger on the side to graze on between bites of rich stew.

Hayashi Rice

Serves 4 to 6

Hayashi is a straight-up beef stew in the tradition of old-school meaty braises like beef bourguignon, served over rice. To be honest, I was never a fan of beef stew when I was growing up. But once I had kids of my own and I discovered that sauce plus starch is a formula for getting them to eat dinner, my eyes opened to the utility and deliciousness of beef stew, specifically hayashi.

A classic hayashi rice is made the hard way, with a slowly reduced demi-glace and beef stock. My version is streamlined and dumbed down so it's easy to make in big batches on the weekend and keep in the fridge or freezer for weeknight dinners. The provincial American in me wants to tell you that you can serve this over egg noodles instead of rice, if you like. Chris disagrees, but that's because he didn't grow up eating egg noodles. However, we both agree that you should pour leftover sauce over seared hamburger patties for another classic yoshoku dish: *hambagu* (hamburger steak).

2 pounds boneless beef chuck roast, cut into 2-inch cubes

3 tablespoons all-purpose flour

2 tablespoons vegetable oil, or as needed

1 onion, sliced thick

½ cup dry red wine

1 tablespoon tomato paste

¾ cup diced tomatoes

2 tablespoons ketchup

2 tablespoons Bull-Dog tonkatsu sauce

1 teaspoon kosher salt

½ teaspoon freshly ground black pepper

1 tablespoon honey

FOR SERVING

Steamed rice (page 25)

1. Place the beef in a bowl. Sprinkle the flour over it and toss to coat.

2. Heat a large, deep skillet or Dutch oven over medium-high heat, then coat with 1 tablespoon of the vegetable oil. Working in batches to avoid crowding the pan, brown the beef pieces thoroughly on all sides. Take your time and add more oil as needed. Crowding will cause the meat to steam rather than brown. Spend 15 to 20 minutes getting the pieces to a handsome shade of brown, transferring them to a plate or tray as they finish.

3. If there's a lot of fat in the pan, pour off all but about 1 tablespoon and return the pan to the stove. Add the onion and sauté until slightly softened, about 3 minutes. Add the wine to the pan and use a spatula to dislodge any browned bits from the bottom, then let the wine reduce until the pan is almost completely dry. Stir in the tomato paste and cook, stirring constantly, for 2 minutes.

4. Return the meat and any accumulated juices to the pan and add the diced tomatoes, ketchup, Bull-Dog sauce, salt, pepper, and 1 cup water. Stir to combine and bring to a simmer, then drop the heat to low, cover, and cook for 1½ to 2 hours, until the meat is fork-tender. I like to give things a stir at the 30- and then the 60-minute mark, then check for doneness every 15 minutes thereafter.

5. Use a slotted spoon or tongs to transfer the meat to a bowl or plate, doing your best to leave the tomatoes and onion behind. Add the honey to the pan and use a handheld blender to puree the vegetables and liquid into a smooth sauce. (If you don't have a handheld blender, you can do this in batches in a regular blender, then return the sauce to the pan.) Once the sauce is smooth, stir the meat back in.

6. You can serve the stew over steamed rice at this point, but if you let it cool and store it in the fridge, it'll taste even better after a day or two. It will keep in the fridge for a week.

Tofu Coney Island

Serves 4

When we were developing our first menu at Ivan Ramen in New York City, I started toying around with a recipe for pork chili without knowing exactly what I wanted to do with it. In the course of my tinkering, I started adding increasing amounts of mushrooms to the mix, until ultimately I realized that we could lose the meat altogether and not miss it.

With that great vegan(!) chili at our disposal, the chefs and I started thinking about how to deploy it. Eventually we had the idea to spoon it over crisp blocks of fried tofu. It was delicious but still not quite finished, so we started rifling through the kitchen for inspiration. Someone found a bottle of French's yellow mustard in the fridge, and from there, we naturally had to add a scattering of chopped onions to complete the resemblance to a Coney Island chili dog. I tend to hate dishes that have a gimmick, but this just works.

I suppose the tofu makes it loosely Japanese, but I don't feel compelled to defend everything on our menu as directly influenced by Japan. And, after all, Coney Island dogs are actually a Detroit thing—the invention of Greek and Macedonian immigrants who'd passed through New York City on their way to the Midwest. I'm happy to continue that legacy as a Jewish guy from Long Island by way of Japan.

One 14-ounce package firm tofu, cut into 1-inch cubes
¼ cup cornstarch
¼ cup potato starch
6 to 8 cups vegetable oil for deep-frying
Kosher salt
2 cups Miso Mushroom Chili (page 92), warm

FOR SERVING
Yellow ballpark mustard (like French's)
Finely diced onions

1. Gently lay the pieces of tofu on paper towels to dry while you set up your frying station. Combine the cornstarch and potato starch in a bowl. Heat about 4 inches of vegetable oil to 350°F in a deep pot over medium heat. Set a wire rack on a baking sheet or line it with paper towels.

2. Working in batches, dredge the tofu pieces in the starch, shake off the excess, add to the hot oil, and fry until crisp and lightly browned on all sides, about 3 minutes. Use a spider or slotted spoon to fish the tofu pieces out of the oil and set them on the rack or paper towels to drain. Season lightly with salt.

3. Arrange the fried tofu on a plate and spoon the mushroom chili on top. Finish with lots of yellow mustard and plenty of diced onions.

RECIPE CONTINUES

Miso Mushroom Chili

Makes 4 cups

This makes more than you need for the Tofu Coney Island, but you'll want extra.

1 pound button mushrooms, trimmed

¾ cup vegetable oil

1 medium onion, diced

1 teaspoon kosher salt

2 tablespoons minced or grated ginger

1 tablespoon minced garlic

½ cup ketchup

¼ cup liquid from Pickled Garlic (made without katsuobushi if you want to keep this recipe vegan, page 232)

¼ cup red (aka) miso

3 tablespoons sake

3 tablespoons mirin

3½ ounces shimeji (beech) or oyster mushrooms, trimmed

1 tablespoon plus 1 teaspoon fresh lemon juice

1. Pulse the button mushrooms in a food processor until they are uniformly broken up into about ⅛-inch pieces. (You can do this by hand if you don't want to bust out the food processor.)

2. Heat a large skillet or Dutch oven over low heat and add the vegetable oil. Give the oil a moment to heat up, then add the onion and salt and cook, stirring regularly, until the onion is softened and golden, about 30 minutes. Add the ginger and garlic and cook until softened and aromatic, about 3 minutes.

3. Add the button mushrooms, turn the heat up to medium, and cook until the mushrooms have yielded their liquid and the mixture has become more or less dry, 15 minutes or so.

4. Stir in the ketchup, pickled garlic liquid, miso, sake, and mirin, bring to a simmer, and cook for 7 minutes. Add the shimeji mushrooms and lemon juice and cook until the mushrooms are tender, about 5 more minutes. Serve, or cool and store in an airtight container in the fridge for up to a week.

Miso-Buttered Corn

Serves 2 to 4 as a side dish

Corn on the cob is an iconic American food, but people love it in Japan too. Corn is expensive there, though, and it's regarded as a special treat during the summer months. A couple years ago, Ivan Ramen was asked to participate in an outdoor festival along the West Side Highway in New York City. With a noodle shop, it's sometimes hard to come up with things to serve for big events, but in this case, we knew immediately what to do. Since it was summertime and the event took place outside, we served ears of grilled corn slathered with butter and miso and coated with a flurry of furikake seasoning. People lost their minds over it.

I've adjusted this recipe for home cooks, for whom it's probably more convenient to slice the corn kernels off the cob and cook them in a pan. Just be sure to use super-fresh, sweet summer corn.

4 ears fresh corn, husked
2 tablespoons vegetable oil
1 teaspoon kosher salt
1 tablespoon minced garlic
2 tablespoons sake
2 tablespoons mirin
2 tablespoons white (shiro) miso
1 tablespoon rice vinegar
1 tablespoon unsalted butter

FOR SERVING
Furikake, store-bought or your
   choice of homemade (page 236
   or 237)
Sliced scallions

1. One at a time, stand the ears of corn up in a flat-bottomed bowl or other container and slice the kernels off the cob. (The container will catch the kernels as they fall.)

2. Heat a large skillet over high heat, then coat with 1 tablespoon of the vegetable oil. Add the corn, season with the salt, and sauté until the kernels begin to brown along the edges, about 5 minutes. Transfer to a bowl.

3. Return the skillet to medium heat and coat with the remaining 1 tablespoon vegetable oil. Add the garlic and cook, stirring, until softened but not browned. Deglaze with the sake and mirin (bearing in mind that the alcohol can catch fire if the pan is very hot). Add the miso, rice vinegar, and butter and whisk to dissolve the miso.

4. Return the corn to the pan and toss to coat the kernels in the sauce. Transfer to a serving plate and garnish with furikake and sliced scallions.

Pork and Tofu Meatballs with Buttermilk Sauce

Serves 6 to 8 as an hors d'oeuvre

My second extended stint in Japan began just as the entire New York restaurant scene was being turned on its head by the rise of chefs like David Chang and April Bloomfield. I watched with interest from afar as the way people ate back home became more like the way it is in Asia: less formal, more joyful, funkier, porkier. Much porkier. I think the popularity of Chang's pork buns ultimately led to pork belly prices rising across the country.

A couple years later, as I was preparing to come back to New York to open my first Stateside ramen shop, I decided I needed a pork meatball on the menu. Everybody was going gaga for meatballs, and I wanted to make my own version. That impulse sent me down a long rabbit hole of testing. At the end of the day, this meatball is probably one of the most researched and tested dishes I've ever made.

The breakthrough came when I was eating at Kotaro, one of my favorite izakayas in Tokyo. One of chef Kotaro-san's signature dishes is a deep-fried panko-crusted meatball that is so bafflingly juicy, it's almost like biting into a soup dumpling. (Usually he serves each diner half a meatball because it's so rich, but when I brought Chris in for dinner, Kotaro-san took one look at my big Chinese friend and served him a whole meatball.) Kotaro's meatball is the inspiration for this one, which I make lighter by adding tofu and serve with two different sauces and a pinch of katsuobushi.

½ onion

7 garlic cloves, peeled

One 3-inch piece ginger, peeled

2 tablespoons soy sauce

½ teaspoon kosher salt

2 large eggs

1 pound ground pork

¼ package (3½ ounces) soft tofu

2½ cups panko

6 to 8 cups vegetable oil for deep-frying

FOR SERVING

Buttermilk Sauce (opposite)

Bull-Dog tonkatsu sauce

Katsuobushi (bonito flakes)

1. Combine the onion, garlic, ginger, soy sauce, and salt in a food processor and process until smooth. Throw in the eggs and whir for 10 more seconds. Pour the mixture into a bowl and add the ground pork, tofu, and 1½ cups of the panko. Mix thoroughly by hand, cover with plastic wrap, and refrigerate for at least 4 hours or overnight.

2. The next day, pulse the remaining 1 cup panko in the food processor until you have a coarse meal, about 15 seconds. Transfer to a shallow container. Retrieve the meatball mixture from the fridge and roll it into 1-ounce (golfball–size) balls.

3. Heat 4 inches of vegetable oil to 325°F in a deep pot over medium heat. Roll each meatball in the panko meal, shake off any excess, and fry for 5 minutes, or until deeply browned and fully cooked through.

4. Transfer the meatballs to a platter and top each one with a spoonful of buttermilk sauce, a squeeze of Bull-Dog sauce, and a few flakes of katsuobushi. Serve as an hors d'oeuvre.

Buttermilk Sauce

Makes about ⅔ cup

¼ cup sour cream

3 tablespoons Kewpie mayonnaise

2 tablespoons buttermilk

1 tablespoon white (shiro) miso

1½ teaspoons aonori (powdered dried green seaweed)

½ teaspoon wasabi paste (from a tube is fine)

Whisk everything together in a bowl. Transfer to an airtight container. The sauce can be refrigerated for up to 2 days.

Smoked Fish Donburi

Serves 1 (multiply as needed)

When I was growing up, my parents lacked any food traditions, save for perhaps one. Almost every Sunday, I could count on the dining table being set up with smoked fish, bagels, cream cheese, and sliced tomatoes and red onions. When I returned from Japan to open my first ramen shop in New York, I wanted to make something that evoked my one true childhood food memory. Donburi is a classic item at ramen shops in Japan—a bowl of rice topped with one or two things to fill out the meal. This dish—a rice bowl of Jewish smoked fish seasoned with sweet tare and furikake—is the truest example of fusion I've ever made.

In New York City, everyone knows what smoked whitefish is (hot-smoked chub from the Great Lakes) and where to find it. It's less widely available outside New York, but nobody will be upset if you substitute hot-smoked (kippered) salmon.

2 cups steamed rice (page 25), still warm

2 tablespoons furikake, store-bought or your choice of homemade (page 236 or 237)

3 to 4 ounces smoked whitefish or hot-smoked salmon, flaked

2 tablespoons ikura (cured salmon roe) or regular salmon roe (optional)

2 tablespoons Sweet Tare (recipe follows)

1 scallion, sliced thin

2 shiso leaves, cut into ribbons (optional)

Stir together the rice and furikake in a bowl. Transfer to a serving bowl and top with the smoked fish. If you've got some ikura on hand, spoon it into the center of the bowl. Drizzle the tare over everything, garnish with the scallion and shiso leaves, and serve.

Sweet Tare (Seasoning Sauce)

Makes about ¾ cup

Tare is a term for a broad range of seasoning sauces, usually soy-based. Sweet tare is also delicious tossed with cooked greens like Chinese broccoli.

⅓ cup soy sauce

2 tablespoons mirin

1 tablespoon plus 1 teaspoon sake

2 teaspoons honey

⅓ cup sugar

¼ cup Dashi (page 28)

Combine the soy sauce, mirin, sake, honey, and sugar in a small saucepan and bring to a simmer over medium heat, stirring to dissolve the sugar. Simmer for 2 minutes, then remove from the heat and stir in the dashi. Allow to cool to room temperature and store for up to 4 days in the fridge.

Bagels with Japanese-ish Fixings

Serves 6

For much of the time we were living in Japan, my wife, Mari, worked as a prop stylist, so she had a lot of friends in the publishing business, including a magazine editor named Yukiko Yamauchi. Yamauchi-san lived a few blocks away, and every time we'd have her over for dinner, she'd bring a plate of home-baked goodies. They were invariably delicious, and, eventually, Yamauchi-san started talking about quitting her job to open a bakery—specifically, a bagel shop.

With a little advice here and there from me, Yamauchi-san opened a shop called Kepo Bagel that has become one of the most popular places in Tokyo. Rather than emulating the big, fluffy New York bagels that you see at places like Ess-a-Bagel, she created her own thing. Her bagels are relatively flat, but they have appropriate sheen and crunch and chew—closer to an old-school NYC bagel than a modern one. I love them.

From time to time, I'll serve this Japanese-inflected bagel spread in her honor. If you make your own bagels, you can take this to the next level by topping them with furikake in place of "everything" seasoning. If not, cream cheese with aonori (powdered dried green seaweed) and shiso gravlax will immensely improve store-bought bagels.

BAGELS
1 or 2 bagels per person, split

TOPPINGS
1½ cups Aonori Cream Cheese (recipe follows)

1 pound Shiso Gravlax (recipe follows), sliced thin

½ red onion, sliced thin

6 to 8 shiso leaves, cut into ribbons

Furikake, store-bought or your choice of homemade (page 236 or 237)

Set out a spread of the sliced bagels and toppings and let people do as they please.

Aonori Cream Cheese
Makes 1½ cups

12 ounces cream cheese, softened

3 tablespoons aonori (powdered dried green seaweed)

Use a spoon or spatula to mix the cream cheese and aonori together in a bowl. This will keep, covered, in the fridge for a few days.

Shiso Gravlax
Makes 1 pound

1 pound skin-on salmon fillet, as fresh and beautiful as possible

⅔ cup packed brown sugar

⅓ cup kosher salt

1 cup loosely packed sliced shiso leaves

1. Using tweezers, carefully remove any pin bones from the salmon fillet. Find a deep baking dish or plastic container that holds the fish snugly.

2. Combine the sugar, salt, and shiso in a bowl. Sprinkle a ½-inch layer of the mixture in the baking dish and lay the salmon on top, skin side down. Pack the fish in the rest of the salt-sugar-shiso mixture and cover loosely with a large piece of plastic wrap. You need to weight down the salmon, which you can go about in a couple different ways: A) If you have a dish or container that is slightly smaller than the one the salmon is sitting in, set the smaller container on top of the fish and weight it down with a few cans or a brick; B) Alternatively, fill a large zip-top bag three-quarters full

with cold water and seal. Nestle the bag over the piece of fish. If the bag hangs over the sides of the baking dish, pour out some of the water and reseal. In either case, wrap the whole apparatus tightly in plastic wrap and allow the fish to cure in the refrigerator for 1 day.

3. After a day, unwrap the fish and flip it over, being sure all the flesh comes into contact with the curing mix (which should be mostly liquid at this point). Weight the fish down again and wrap it again in fresh plastic. Cure in the fridge for 3 or 4 more days, depending

on the thickness of your fillet. The gravlax is ready when the fish is firm to the touch.

4. Wipe the cure off the salmon and wrap it in clean plastic wrap. Refrigerate until ready to serve. It will keep for up to a week.

Sushi-Ginger Pizza Bites

Makes 1 mini pizza (multiply as you see fit and serve as an hors d'oeuvre)

I know this recipe sounds insane, but I assure you it's amazing.

Before we go any further, though, let me state for the record that some of the world's best pizza makers work in Tokyo. This recipe has nothing to do with great pizza, but I don't want you thinking that all Japanese pizza is bonkers.

Anyway, about ten years ago, my wife came home from dinner one night raving about how the chef had developed these clever izakaya dishes, and how surprisingly delicious everything was. One of the things she loved most was a pizza topped with sushi ginger. I wrote it off as stoner food and forgot about it until a recent evening when we found ourselves with a bunch of leftover gyoza skins. Mari said, "Hey, why don't we try making that sushi-ginger pizza on gyoza wrappers?"

We popped a few in the oven and, miraculously, the combination of sushi ginger and cheese didn't freak me out. In fact, it was outstanding. Try it for yourself at home with plenty of ice-cold beer (or, you know, a joint).

FOR EACH PIZZA

1 round gyoza wrapper

½ teaspoon Kewpie mayonnaise

Pinch of shichimi togarashi

Pinch of kosher salt

Pinch of katsuobushi (bonito flakes)

1 slice pickled sushi ginger, cut into thin strips

1 tablespoon shredded mozzarella

1. Heat the oven or toaster oven to 400°F. Line a baking sheet with foil.

2. For each pizza, lay a gyoza wrapper on the foil, spread with Kewpie mayo, and then season with togarashi and salt. Crush the katsuobushi between your fingers and sprinkle it on top. Strew the sushi ginger over the pizza and top with mozzarella cheese.

3. Slide the pan into the oven and bake until the gyoza wrappers have crisped and the cheese is gooey and beginning to brown, about 5 minutes. Allow to cool for a minute before serving.

SANDWICHES

Of all the magnificent things to eat in Tokyo, the one that seems to make the most lasting impact on first-time visitors is the humble sandwich (*sando*). It was that way for Chris the first time I took him to Japan. Every night after dinner (or a second dinner), he'd stop in at a Lawson's or Family Mart convenience store and buy a *katsu* (pork cutlet) or egg sandwich as a midnight snack.

I think there are several things at play here. First, there's a bit of novelty and nostalgia involved. Sandwiches in Japan are first cousins to the Wonder Bread ones you ate from a paper bag as a kid. Second, and more important, Japanese sandwiches are incredibly delicious.

The iconic Japanese sandwich is a crustless white bread sandwich, cut in half diagonally and wrapped in plastic. Nothing about it sounds especially impressive, but it is a thing of true and enduring beauty. Squishy-soft and chock-full of umami, its appeal is primal. Even purchased from the refrigerated shelves at convenience stores (*conbini*), they're somehow never stale.

There's nothing complicated about making a Japanese sandwich, but it's worth familiarizing yourself with the basic components:

MILK BREAD (SHOKUPAN): Some of the best breads—and pastries—I've ever encountered were baked in Japan, and certainly not all Japanese sandwiches come on spongy white bread, but shokupan is the iconic sandwich bread. It's a close relative to the white bread we know in America, slightly sweet and pillowy soft. And though I usually find the practice crass, we always slice the crusts off the bread when we make these sandwiches. It worked in elementary school, and it works here.

KEWPIE MAYO: The lord of all mayonnaise. Eggier and richer than American mayo, with a healthy dose of umami courtesy of MSG.

BULL-DOG TONKATSU SAUCE: Tangy, sweet, and salty, Bull-Dog sauce cuts through the richness of fried foods and gives a little burst of brightness to tori katsu (chicken cutlet) and menchi katsu (beef croquette) sandwiches.

Egg Salad Sandwich

Makes 1 sandwich

2 large eggs

2 tablespoons Kewpie mayonnaise

Kosher salt

2 slices Japanese milk bread
(shokupan) or other white bread,
crusts removed

1. Bring 5 cups water to a boil in a small saucepan and gently lower in the eggs. Cook for 8½ minutes, then drain and peel under cold running water.

2. Place the eggs in a bowl and use a fork or knife to slice/mash them into small pieces. Mix with the Kewpie and season to taste with salt. Make a sandwich.

Scrambled Egg Sandwich

Makes 1 sandwich

2 large eggs

½ teaspoon sugar

¼ teaspoon kosher salt

1 tablespoon unsalted butter

2 slices Japanese milk bread
(shokupan) or other white bread,
crusts removed

1 to 2 tablespoons Kewpie
mayonnaise

Whisk the eggs in a small bowl, then whisk in the sugar and salt. Set a small skillet over medium-low heat and add the butter. Once the butter is melted, add the eggs and cook, stirring and folding constantly, until they are barely cooked and still jiggly. Slather both pieces of bread with the mayonnaise, then sandwich the eggs between them.

Chicken Cutlet (Tori Katsu) Sandwich

Makes 2 sandwiches

1 boneless, skinless chicken breast (about 12 ounces)

1 teaspoon kosher salt

¼ cup all-purpose flour

1 large egg

¾ cup panko

About ½ cup vegetable oil

4 slices Japanese milk bread (shokupan) or other white bread, crusts removed

2 to 3 tablespoons Kewpie mayonnaise

2 tablespoons Bull-Dog tonkatsu sauce

1. Slice the chicken breast horizontally in half, giving you 2 fillets, each about ½ inch thick. Season with the salt.

2. Set up a breading station by lining up three shallow trays—pie tins work well—and filling them with the flour, egg, and panko, respectively. Lightly beat the egg. One at a time, coat each piece of chicken with flour, gently dusting off any excess, then give it a dip in the egg and, finally, a coating of panko. Don't be stingy with the bread crumbs—cover the whole piece of chicken and press down gently to ensure a good coating.

3. Fill a medium skillet with ¼ inch of oil and heat over medium heat to about 350°F. You can tell that the oil is ready if you toss a few panko crumbs into the oil and they immediately begin to sizzle. Carefully slide one piece of chicken into the oil and fry, turning once, until golden brown, about 3 minutes per side. Transfer to a paper towel or wire rack to drain while you fry the other piece.

4. Trim the chicken pieces to fit the pieces of bread (eat the trimmings), then slather each slice of bread with mayo and Bull-Dog sauce and sandwich the chicken between them.

Beef Croquette (Menchi Katsu) Sandwich

Makes 1 sandwich

2 slices Japanese milk bread (shokupan) or other white bread, crusts removed

1 Beef Croquette (Menchi Katsu, page 166), fresh or day-old

1 to 2 tablespoons Kewpie mayonnaise

1 tablespoon Bull-Dog tonkatsu sauce

Toast both slices of bread. If your menchi katsu is a day old, you can reheat it in the toaster oven with the bread, but honestly, it's going to be delicious cold out of the fridge. Slather both slices of toast with the mayo and Bull-Dog sauce, then sandwich the katsu in between, breaking it up into pieces as necessary to make it fit.

Empathy

Cures for What Ails You

Since moving back to the States after my family's most recent decade-long period in Tokyo, I often think about the effect that Japan had on me. What did I learn? What behavioral traits have I held on to? What can I pass on to my children?

I like to believe that even living in New York, my family continues to subscribe to the Japanese practice of *meiwaku o kakenai*. Simply put, it's the art of not getting in other people's way. Picture an invisible bubble extending four feet around you. A Japanese person takes responsibility for anything that happens in his or her bubble. If there's trash on the ground, they pick it up. If they need to cough or yawn or stretch, they consider how doing so might affect someone else.

That notion goes hand in hand with *kuuki o yomu*, "reading the air." Japanese people are sensitive to the social situations they're in. They're aware of the mood in the room, and their effect on it. Once again, I'm generalizing—there are plenty of rude, oblivious people in Japan—but when most of the people in a society show the same concern, the overall quality of life rises. I was chastised mercilessly by neighbors and trash collectors when I first moved to Japan for not dealing with my garbage properly on collection day. At first I was indignant. If someone in New York were to lecture me about how I threw my trash out, I would have told them to fuck off. But then again, relative to Tokyo, New York is filthy. And there's the rub. Life in a crowded, hectic city is only livable if everybody plays ball. In Tokyo, a city of fourteen million people, the streets are clean and you never take an elbow to the ribs from some idiot blindly swinging his arms while he walks.

Top left: If Tokyo can keep their parks this clean, why can't we?
Top right: Family dinner at a yakitori place in Kichijoji.
Bottom right: Orderliness prevails in the streets.
Bottom left: After all these years, I still follow Mari's lead in the subways.

That's not to say I instantaneously became a great person. I'm a work in progress. The first time my wife and I were riding a train in Tokyo together, I was sitting with my legs stretched out in front of me. Mari slapped my thigh and told me to pull them in. My inner New Yorker was like, *What the fuck? The train's empty.* But that's not the point. If you want to maintain a certain kind of behavior, you have to do it all the time—even when the train's empty.

The sort of vigilant courtesy I'm talking about is often confused by Americans with standoffishness. But more often than not, what you're witnessing is an overabundance of empathy. If you're at a party in Japan where you don't know anybody, very rarely will you be allowed to sit in a corner by yourself looking miserable. Someone is going to grab you and bring you into what's happening. It's called *giri*—a big-brotherly obligation to your fellow person—and once you experience it, you feel obliged to pass it on even if you're not naturally inclined to be outgoing.

What does this have to do with food, Ivan? Fair question.

Growing up, I desperately wanted food and love to be intertwined, but my mother was uncooperative. Nothing she fed us had anything to do with feeling good, except for maybe Campbell's cream of mushroom soup when we were sick or a bagel and lox on Sunday mornings. So when I moved to Japan after college, young and alone and aimless, I latched on to the food in Tokyo on a deep emotional level. To this day, when I'm sick or feeling miserable, the things I eat to feel better are almost all Japanese: rice and noodle dishes, meat and

vegetables slowly cooked in sweetened soy sauce, hot pots.

I don't think it's a huge stretch to say that the extraordinary degree of concern for others I've witnessed in Japan translates to a cuisine capable of truly nourishing the body and soul. I think that comfort food in the West often gets conflated with junk food. The dishes in this chapter will warm and restore you, but they won't weigh you down. It's not health food, but you feel healthier after eating it.

If you need more evidence that Japanese cooks excel at making comfort food, take a look at the donabe. One of the world's most ideal comfort-

cooking vessels is the ceramic pot, and some of the most beautiful but functional clay pots come from Japan. Donabe distribute heat evenly and are as useful for gently cooking things like rice and fish as they are for quicker-cooking meals like Sukiyaki (page 139). At our house, we rely on a big donabe (3 quarts) to feed our family of five throughout the colder months.

In addition to some of the classic dishes that have brought me comfort through the years, this chapter includes a handful of great donabe recipes. If you don't have a donabe, an enamel-coated cast-iron pot or Dutch oven will work fine.

Above: My wife has been essential to my understanding of kuuki o yomu, but I've still got a long way to go.
Opposite: Friendly greeters outside a cafe in Ueno.

Rice with Tea or Broth (Ochazuke)

Serves 1 (multiply as needed)

Ochazuke—rice immersed in hot tea or dashi—is a delicate, restorative dish that can be assembled with a wide array of toppings. It's a terrific way to pull together a snack from leftovers, or you can go a more indulgent route with fresh fish and seafood. But ochazuke can easily be kept vegetarian by topping it with things like Seasoned Spinach (Ohitashi, page 204) or Seasoned Shiitake Mushrooms (Shiitake no Amakara ni, page 199), and shio kombu (salted seaweed). Whatever you choose to do, the beauty of ochazuke is that it looks and tastes like something you'd eat at a fancy kaiseki restaurant, but it's unbelievably simple to make.

RICE

You can make a fresh batch, but this dish was originally intended to use up yesterday's rice. Either way, make sure the rice is warm so it doesn't cool down the broth too much.

⅔ cup steamed rice (page 25), fresh or warmed leftovers

TOPPINGS

Choose as many as you like.

1 serving (2 ounces) Broiled Salmon (recipe follows)

2 Seasoned Shiitake Mushrooms (Shiitake no Amakara ni, page 199), sliced thin

1 tablespoon Seasoned Spinach (Ohitashi, page 204)

1 tablespoon shio kombu (shredded salted seaweed)

4 thin slices takuan (pickled daikon)

3 shiso leaves, sliced into ribbons

1 to 2 umeboshi (pickled plums), pitted and torn into smallish pieces

1 tablespoon shredded nori

BROTH

1 cup Japanese green tea (sencha, genmaicha, gyokuro, hojicha, etc.) or Dashi of your choice (page 28), or a blend of the two, kept hot until the last second

1. Scoop the rice into a medium bowl and arrange your chosen toppings around and on top of it.

2. Pour the tea and/or dashi on top to heat everything through. You can add more broth or toppings if you'd like.

Broiled Salmon

Makes 5 servings

One 10-ounce skinless salmon fillet
1 teaspoon kosher salt

1. Season the salmon with the salt and let it sit at room temp for 30 minutes.

2. Fire up the broiler in your oven or toaster oven. Place the salmon on a foil-lined baking sheet and slide it into the oven, 3 to 4 inches from the broiler. Cook for 5 to 7 minutes, depending on the thickness of the fillet, flipping the fish about halfway through cooking and watching carefully to avoid burning. Remove the salmon from the oven when it's medium-rare, wrap it in the foil, and let cool to room temperature.

3. Use your fingers or a fork to break the salmon into flakes. Store for up to 2 days in the fridge.

Rice Porridge (Ojiya)

Serves 2

Rice porridge is common in many Asian cultures and countries, where it's often eaten at breakfast. But, once again proving that I'm not really Japanese, I don't usually eat it in the morning. Ojiya is what I eat when I'm feeling down in the dumps. If I'm sick, or if Mari or one of the kids has the flu or a fever, a pot of ojiya immediately goes on the stove. We always have leftover rice on hand, which makes preparing the dish much easier, but it's no trouble to start from raw rice—simply cook the rice longer and add more water.

To the uninitiated, a bowl of ojiya might seem bland. Think of it as a canvas. You can leave it plain and appreciate its creaminess and subtle rice flavor, or dress it up as extravagantly as you want. If you're laid up sick, a tiny dash of shoyu is probably all you can stomach. If you're on the mend, add more toppings.

2 cups steamed rice (page 25)

1 cup Dashi (page 28)

2 teaspoons soy sauce

½ teaspoon kosher salt

1 large egg, beaten

FOR SERVING

Choose as many as you like:

Sliced negi (Japanese green onions) or scallions

Katsuobushi (bonito flakes)

Soy sauce

Yukari (shiso rice seasoning)

Japanese chili oil (rayu) or Chunky Chili Oil (page 234)

1. Combine the rice, dashi, and 1 cup water in a saucepan and bring to a simmer over medium-high heat. Drop the heat to low and cook at a very gentle simmer, stirring occasionally, until most of the liquid has been absorbed or evaporated, about 8 minutes. Add another cup of water and cook, stirring occasionally, until the rice has broken down into a thick porridge, about 10 minutes. (If you like your porridge even mushier, you can add more water and cook it longer.)

2. Stir in the soy sauce and salt. Remove the pan from the heat and stir in the beaten egg. Divide between two bowls and garnish as desired.

Clay Pot Mixed Rice (Takikomi Gohan)

Two ways

Like the majority of people on earth, I find incredible comfort in a bowl of perfectly cooked, unadorned white rice. But if you don't get quite the same joy from plain rice as I do, these recipes add a little bit of texture and umami without displacing rice as the star. They're only two examples of a simple and versatile rice-cooking technique: Soak rice in a flavorful liquid, add some seasonal accoutrements that will stand up to hard cooking, and steam everything together in one pot. In Japanese, mixed-rice dishes like this fall under the umbrella term *takikomi gohan*.

If you own an electric or cast-iron rice cooker or earthenware donabe—hell, even a heavy-bottomed saucepan will do—you can start experimenting with this basic idea. The following are two takes on takikomi gohan—one vegetarian and one for omnivores. (For a fancier take on this technique, see the recipe for Tai Meshi—a whole fish cooked in dashi-flavored rice—in the New Year's chapter, page 213.)

The following recipes are designed for a 1½-quart rice cooker (I use a cast-iron one made by Staub), but you can easily use a larger pot and increase the recipe for a crowd.

Shimeji Mushroom Rice (Kinoko no Takikomi Gohan)

Serves 4

Here I'm keeping things on the simpler side by adding a pile of shimeji (beech) mushrooms to rice flavored with soy and sake.

1½ cups Japanese short-grain rice

3 tablespoons soy sauce

2 tablespoons mirin

2 tablespoons sake

¼ cup loosely packed katsuobushi (bonito flakes), finely chopped (optional)

3 ounces shimeji (beech) mushrooms, trimmed

GARNISHES

3 scallions, chopped

3 shiso leaves, cut into ribbons

One 1-inch piece ginger, peeled and cut into matchsticks

2 umeboshi (pickled plums), pitted and minced (optional)

Shredded nori

1. Place the rice in a fine-mesh strainer and rinse under cold water, using your fingers to agitate the rice, until the water runs almost clear. (Alternatively, place the rice in a pot or bowl and rinse and drain away the water three times.)

2. Transfer the rice to a 1½-quart enamel-glazed cast-iron pot (or similarly sized saucepan or donabe) and add the soy sauce, mirin, sake, and 1¼ cups water. Sprinkle the katsuobushi, if using, over the top. Let the rice soak for at least 20 minutes or up to 1 hour.

3. Once the rice has soaked, separate the mushrooms from one another and add them to the pot. Bring to a simmer over medium heat, stirring occasionally to prevent sticking or clumping. Then cover the pot, drop the heat to low, and set a timer for 14 minutes.

(While the rice cooks, you can prepare the garnishes.)

4. After 14 minutes, uncover the rice and fluff with a fork or spoon. Cover again and let stand for 5 minutes before stirring in the garnishes and serving.

Chicken and Vegetable Rice (Tori no Takikomi Gohan)

Serves 4

Here's a more action-packed take on Takikomi Gohan (page 116)—a one-pot meal of rice, dark chicken meat, mushrooms, carrots, and burdock root. If you can't find burdock or don't like it, try parsnips or turnips.

1½ cups Japanese short-grain rice

2 tablespoons soy sauce

2 tablespoons mirin

2 tablespoons sake

1 teaspoon kosher salt

¼ cup loosely packed katsuobushi (bonito flakes), finely chopped

2 ounces burdock root (gobo) or other hearty root vegetable, peeled and cut into thin matchsticks

1 small carrot, peeled and sliced ⅛ inch thick on the bias

12 ounces boneless, skinless chicken thighs, cut into 1-inch pieces

3 ounces shimeji (beech) mushrooms, trimmed

1. Place the rice in a fine-mesh strainer and rinse under cold water, using your fingers to agitate the rice, until the water runs almost clear. (Alternatively, place the rice in a pot or bowl and rinse and drain away the water three times.)

2. Transfer the rice to a 1½-quart enamel-glazed cast-iron pot (or similarly sized heavy saucepan or earthenware donabe) and add the soy sauce, mirin, sake, salt, and 1¼ cups water. Sprinkle the chopped katsuobushi over the top. Let the rice soak for at least 20 minutes or up to 1 hour.

3. Once the rice has soaked, add the burdock and carrot, and then the chicken. Separate the shimeji mushrooms from one another and add them. Bring the water to a simmer over medium heat, then cover the pot, drop the heat to low, and set a timer for 14 minutes.

4. After 14 minutes, uncover the rice and fluff with a fork or spoon. Cover again and let stand for 5 minutes before serving.

Pork and Miso-Ginger Stew (Tonjiru)

Serves 4

Every family I know in Japan has its own recipe for tonjiru. It's cold-weather home cooking of the best kind: quick and simple and infinitely customizable. At its core, it's just miso soup with pork, but you can build it out with whatever vegetables you like. Root vegetables take especially well to the flavor of the sweet, meaty broth, so it's a brilliant way to get pickier kids to eat more carrots, potatoes, turnips, and daikon.

You can make tonjiru with water, dashi, or chicken stock, depending on what you have on hand. Waiting until the very end to add a hit of ginger gives the soup a ton of sweet aroma and cooks the ginger just enough so that you're not punched in the mouth with its spice.

1 small (8 ounces) daikon, peeled

1 medium (8 ounces) sweet potato, preferably Japanese, peeled

3 medium carrots, peeled

1 pound thinly sliced skinless pork belly (see Thinly Sliced Meat, page 129) or uncured bacon, cut into 1-inch pieces

1 tablespoon toasted sesame oil

½ large onion, sliced

4¼ cups Dashi (page 28), chicken stock, or water

½ cup tightly packed katsuobushi (bonito flakes)

½ cup white (shiro) miso

One 3-inch piece ginger, peeled and finely grated

1 teaspoon sugar

One 14-ounce package medium or firm tofu, drained and cut into 1-inch cubes

1. Slice the daikon lengthwise in half, and then into quarters. Slice each piece crosswise into ½-inch-thick quarter moons. Cut the sweet potato into pieces that are roughly the same size. If you've got especially fat carrots, split them lengthwise in half before slicing them into 1-inch lengths. You want everything to cook in the same amount of time, so exercise your judgment.

2. Heat a Dutch oven or other large heavy-bottomed pot over medium heat and add the pork belly or bacon. Cook, stirring, until the meat is mostly cooked through, about 3 minutes. Clear a little space in the pot and add the sesame oil. Let it heat for a moment, then add the onion and cook until it begins to turn translucent, about 3 minutes. Stir in the daikon, sweet potato, and carrot and cook for another 2 to 3 minutes to get rid of some of the rawness.

3. Add the dashi, stock, or water and bring to a gentle simmer. Stuff the katsuobushi into a tea ball, a tea bag, or a sachet made from cheesecloth, and drop it into the soup. Cook until the vegetables are tender, 10 to 15 minutes.

4. Fish out the katsuobushi packet and discard (or empty out the tea ball). Put the miso in a bowl, pour a large ladle of the hot broth over it, and whisk until the miso is completely dissolved. (This method prevents clumps of miso in the soup.) Add the ginger and sugar and whisk once more. Stir the miso mixture into the soup, add the tofu, and simmer for 5 more minutes to heat the tofu through. Serve.

Pork and Root Vegetable Stew with Shirataki Noodles (Niku Jaga)

Serves 4

The name *niku jaga* translates literally as "meat and potatoes," which is probably the most apt way of describing this dish. It is home cooking at its finest (although it's served in lots of restaurants too): cheap cuts of meat, root vegetables, and noodles simmered in a sweet soy broth. When I first moved to Japan, I lived on food like this, and when Mari and I got together, she would often make niku jaga for me.

The only part of this recipe that might be unfamiliar to you are the noodles. Shirataki are a thin, squiggly pasta made from yams. When you first open the package, they have a slightly unpleasant odor that needs to be rinsed away, but their flavor is totally mild. Because they're gluten free, more and more people have discovered them in recent years.

12 ounces (2 packages) **shirataki noodles or fresh ramen noodles**

⅓ cup **soy sauce**

⅓ cup **mirin**

⅓ cup **sake**

1 tablespoon plus 1 teaspoon **sugar**

2 teaspoons **vegetable oil**

8 ounces **thinly sliced skinless pork belly (see Thinly Sliced Meat, page 129) or uncured bacon, cut into 1-inch pieces**

1 medium **onion, sliced thin**

2 large **Yukon Gold potatoes, peeled and cut into bite-size pieces**

2 medium **carrots, sliced into ½-inch-thick pieces on the bias**

1. If using shirataki noodles, bring 2 cups water to a boil in a small saucepan. Meanwhile, place the shirataki noodles in a colander in the sink and rinse with cold water. Pour the boiling water over the noodles to help remove any funky odor.

2. Combine the soy sauce, mirin, sake, and sugar with 2½ cups water in a bowl. Whisk to dissolve the sugar.

3. Heat a Dutch oven or other large heavy-bottomed pot over medium-high heat, then coat with the vegetable oil. Add the pork belly and cook until most of the fat has rendered, about 4 minutes. Add the onion and cook until softened and turning translucent, about 4 minutes. Add the potatoes and carrots and cook for another 3 minutes to remove some of the rawness.

4. Pour in the soy sauce mixture and bring to a simmer, using a wooden spoon to dislodge any bits stuck to the bottom of the pot. Add the rinsed noodles, reduce the heat to medium-low, and cook until the potatoes and carrots are fork-tender, about 20 minutes. (If you're using ramen noodles, add them to the pan about 3 minutes before serving.) Divvy up the stew among bowls and serve warm.

Okinawa-Style Soba with Pork Belly and Katsuobushi (Soki Soba)

Serves 2 as a main dish, 4 as an appetizer

I'm a ramen guy. I appreciate the subtle beauty of soba and udon, but as an American, I'm drawn to noodle soups that are a little punchier. Okinawa-style soba is a bit of a hybrid creation. I had my first bowl of it at an Okinawan restaurant in Tokyo, and I was blown away by how rich and smoky and porky the broth managed to be while staying clean and light. There's a certain set of Japanese flavors that have made a huge impression on me as a gaijin. When I think of comfort food, I think of dashi and soy, and when I come across a dish like this, I perk up immediately. If you, like me, have a Japan-shaped hole in your heart, this dish will revitalize you.

One thing to note is that much will depend on the quality of noodles you buy. In Japan, Okinawa soba noodles resemble thin udon, and they're made with wheat flour, as opposed to buckwheat like most soba. The closest thing you'll find to Okinawa-style soba in the States is dried udon, but you should be able to find good, flavorful dried udon. Once you find noodles you like, stock up.

10 ounces skinless pork belly, cut into 1-inch cubes

4 scallions, white and light green parts sliced into 2-inch lengths, dark green parts sliced thin for garnish

One 2½-inch piece ginger, peeled and sliced thin

3 tablespoons soy sauce

3 tablespoons sake

1 tablespoon sugar

Kosher salt

½ cup tightly packed katsuobushi (bonito flakes), plus more for garnish

6 ounces dried udon

1. Combine the pork belly, white and light green scallion parts, ginger, 2 tablespoons of the soy sauce, the sake, sugar, and 4 cups water in a medium saucepan and bring to a simmer over medium-high heat. Drop the heat to low and simmer for 1 hour and 15 minutes, or until the pork is tender; replenish with water as necessary to maintain the same amount of liquid—about ½ cup every ½ hour.

2. Use a slotted spoon to scoop the meat out of the liquid. Strain the broth, return to the pot, then add the remaining 1 tablespoon soy sauce and season to taste with salt. Add the katsuobushi and let it stand for 10 minutes.

3. Meanwhile, cook the udon according to the package directions.

4. Divide the noodles into two or four bowls. Strain the broth and ladle it over the noodles, then top each with a few pieces of pork belly, sliced scallion greens, and a big pinch of katsuobushi.

Beef and Onion Rice Bowl (Gyudon)

Serves 4

Like most gaijin, my introduction to gyudon came via fast food. I was a twentysomething-year-old kid in Tokyo trying to eat cheaply, and everywhere I looked there was a Yoshinoya restaurant slinging bowls of rice topped with sweet-salty beef and onions. Gyudon is one of the most common dishes in all of Japan, largely thanks to these chains, where you can order it enhanced with everything from scallions to kimchi to cheese. It's a bit of a disservice to gyudon, because the meat at these places isn't exactly A5 wagyu beef, but the ironic beauty of this dish is that it does wonders for cheap meat.

At home I never eat gyudon without an egg—either a raw egg yolk or a seasoned egg smashed in with the rice. I suggest you do the same.

1 large onion, sliced thick

¼ cup plus 1 tablespoon sake

¼ cup plus 1 tablespoon soy sauce

¼ cup plus 1 tablespoon mirin

¼ cup sugar

1 pound thinly sliced beef (preferably chuck roll or a cut that stands up to longish cooking; see Thinly Sliced Meat, page 129)

One 1½-inch piece ginger, peeled and finely grated

FOR SERVING

Steamed rice (page 25)

4 raw egg yolks (of a quality and freshness you feel comfortable eating raw) or Soy-Marinated Eggs (Ajitama, page 30)

Kimchi (optional)

Shichimi togarashi

1. Bring 2 cups water to a simmer in a large skillet over medium-high heat. Add the onion, sake, soy sauce, mirin, and sugar and cook for about 3 minutes, adjusting the heat to maintain a simmer, until the onion is softened slightly.

2. Stir in the sliced beef and bring the liquid back to a simmer, then tilt the pan and use a flat skimmer to remove any gray scum on the surface. Cover and simmer gently for about 20 minutes—the beef should be tender and the onion fully softened. Remove the pan from the heat and stir in the ginger.

3. Serve over steamed rice, ladling a generous amount of broth into each bowl. Garnish each portion with an egg yolk or ajitama, kimchi (if you like), and shichimi togarashi to taste.

Stewed Beef Shank (Gyu Suji Nikomi)

Serves 4

This recipe isn't *technically* for gyu suji nikomi, which is usually made with meaty cuts of tendon, whereas I use beef shank because the right cut of tendon is relatively difficult to come by. Nevertheless, I wanted to include a version of the dish in this book because it is such an immensely comforting thing to eat and also a real source of insight into dining in Japan.

Gyu suji nikomi has all the warm, soul-satisfying characteristics of comfort food, but it's not heavy; you usually eat it as part of a progression of dishes in a restaurant. At an izakaya, you'll order a bevy of light dishes and then finish with a small portion of this rich, delicious stew. It's comfort without the discomfort of overeating.

(If you do want to make the dish with tendon, you can make the broth and use it to cook the tendon in a pressure cooker, then add the vegetables once the meat is fully tender.)

1¾ pounds beef shank, cut into 1-inch-thick slices by the butcher

½ cup sake

½ cup mirin

⅓ cup plus 1 tablespoon soy sauce

1 tablespoon sugar

11 ounces daikon, peeled, quartered lengthwise, and cut into 1-inch-long pieces

About 5 ounces burdock root (gobo; or substitute another hearty root vegetable, such as parsnip or turnip), peeled, halved lengthwise, and cut into 1-inch pieces

½ cup tightly packed katsuobushi (bonito flakes)

One 1-inch piece ginger, peeled and cut into matchsticks

2 medium carrots, peeled and cut into 1-inch pieces

FOR SERVING

Steamed rice (page 25; optional)

1. Place the beef shank in a medium (3- to 4-quart) Dutch oven or other heavy-bottomed pot and cover with 8 cups water. Bring to a simmer over high heat, then lower the heat to medium and use a flat mesh skimmer or ladle to skim any impurities that rise to the surface. There may be a fair amount, so take your time and rinse the skimmer with warm water between dips into the liquid. Then continue to simmer for about 15 minutes.

2. Add the sake, mirin, soy sauce, and sugar, turn the heat down to low, cover the pot, and simmer gently for about 1 hour.

3. Add the daikon and burdock to the pot and cook for another 30 minutes, or until the meat is tender. Pull the beef out of the pot with a pair of tongs, use a fork and knife to break the meat into smaller chunks, and return the meat to the pot.

4. Stuff the katsuobushi into a tea ball, a tea bag, or a cheesecloth sachet and drop it into the pot. Let stand for 10 minutes with the pot uncovered, then remove the katsuobushi.

5. Add the ginger and carrots, cover the pot again, and simmer for about 20 minutes, until all of the vegetables are tender. Serve the broth, meat, and vegetables together, with bowls of steamed rice on the side, if you like.

ΝΑΒΕ
[HOT POTS]

Nabe are multipurpose Japanese cooking vessels that have given rise to an entire class of dishes unto themselves (*nabemono*). They can vary in shape and specific function, but in general we're talking about heavy, wide ceramic (*donabe*) or cast-iron (*tetsunabe*) pots. Functionally, they're a bit like shallow Dutch ovens. They're ideal for simmering and steaming, but you can cook anything in a nabe, from rice to stews and soups to stir-fries to hot pots.

Every two or three weeks during the colder months, my family will gather around a big nabe for a warm, nourishing dinner. There are dozens of different nabe dishes that make their way through our rotation, but this chapter includes some of our favorites. I love them because not only are they wholesome and tasty, but they're also relatively painless to put together. You prep all your ingredients, and they all go into the pot. A nabe is also my preferred way of cooking and serving high-quality beef, as with Sukiyaki (Beef Hot Pot, page 139), which is slightly more involved than other nabe dishes and more of a special-occasion dish for us.

Don't stress out if you don't own a nabe that meets the same specifications as mine (a 3-quart ceramic donabe). A good Dutch oven, or even a deep, heavy skillet, makes a fine substitute.

THINLY SLICED MEAT

A good number of recipes in this book call for thinly sliced meat (pork belly or beef). If you're not accustomed to shopping in Asian markets or cooking Japanese food, you might be scratching your head about what exactly we mean by "thinly sliced." When it comes to pork belly, I'm talking about bacon-esque slices. (In fact, uncured bacon makes a perfectly reasonable substitute.) For dishes like sukiyaki and Gyudon (Beef and Onion Rice Bowl, page 125), you want extremely thin pieces of fatty beef. "Paper-thin" would be an overstatement, but nothing you're going to find in the meat case of your standard American supermarket is quite right either. You want rib-eye or chuck shaved a little thinner than you'd like your pastrami and a little thicker than you want your turkey. Let's call it $1/8$ inch. (See the next page for examples.)

A good Japanese market will sell packages of presliced meat labeled with their intended use: shabu shabu, sukiyaki, gyudon, and so on. (These packaged meats also usually come in different grades, if you feel like splurging for the good stuff.) If you don't have access to a Japanese market, you can try asking the butcher at your meat counter to shave a boneless roast thin on the meat slicer for you. However, not every meat counter has a meat slicer. Don't despair. You can buy a piece of the meat you need and pop it into the freezer for an hour so it's easier to slice, then cut your own thin slices. The result might not be as perfect as what you'd find at a Japanese market, but it'll still be tasty.

Every-Night Hot Pot (Jouya Nabe)

Serves 4

This is a classic, uncomplicated nabe of pork belly, mushrooms, and cabbage that you can prepare in half an hour if you happen to have a quart of dashi in the fridge. There's very little going on here ingredients-wise, but the resulting broth is surprisingly rich and flavorful without being heavy. It's a clean-tasting dish and proof that ponzu, which is now available in most large supermarkets, is one of the world's great condiments. Bring the whole pot out to the table and let everyone season their own serving of meat, vegetables, and broth.

If you don't have dashi on hand, this recipe is still incredibly easy—it'll just take a little more time to infuse the cooking liquid with a piece of kombu.

One 5-inch square piece kombu or 4½ cups Dashi (page 28)

1 pound thinly sliced skinless pork belly (see Thinly Sliced Meat, page 129) or uncured bacon

8 ounces napa cabbage

About 5 ounces (1 package) enoki mushrooms, trimmed

FOR SERVING

Ponzu sauce

Soy sauce

Shichimi togarashi

Steamed rice (page 25)

1. Combine the kombu and 5 cups cold water in a large (3- to 5-quart) nabe, Dutch oven, or braiser and let the seaweed soak for at least 30 minutes or up to 1 hour. Or, if you have 4½ cups dashi at the ready, skip ahead to step 2.

2. Meanwhile, prep the meat and vegetables: Slice the pork belly or bacon into 3-inch-long pieces. Core the cabbage and cut it into 3-inch pieces. Break up the mushrooms into five or six smaller bundles.

3. Bring the water and kombu, if using, to a gentle simmer over medium heat and cook for 10 minutes, then remove the kombu. (Or simply bring the dashi to a simmer.) Add the pork, cabbage, and mushrooms to the pot, cover, and simmer for 15 minutes, or until the cabbage and mushrooms are tender and the pork is cooked through.

4. Serve family-style, with ponzu, soy sauce, and shichimi togarashi on the side. To eat, start with a splash of ponzu, then add some soy sauce and togarashi if you want it a little spicier and saltier. Steamed rice makes this a well-rounded meal.

Chicken Hot Pot (Mizutaki)

Serves 4 to 6

Mizutaki has made regular appearances in our house ever since Mari and I shared one at our friend's restaurant Mizutaki Tojiro, in Tokyo. Dinner at Mizutaki Tojiro begins with an array of otsumami—small plates of fried things, crunchy salads, and other specialties meant to be eaten with drinks—but the main event is the mizutaki. Out from the kitchen comes a cauldron of rich, flavorful chicken stock with half a dozen chicken legs bobbing around. Everybody gets a little ramekin of salt and another one of ponzu. It's so basic that you're skeptical, but then you taste it and you're overwhelmed by how incredibly satisfying it is. It's like being inside a chicken. That may sound horrible, but I mean it in a good way.

At our house, we add some vegetables and Chicken Meatballs (Tsukune, page 182) to fill out the meal. Use the highest-quality chicken you can find. And if you happen to have homemade chicken stock in the fridge, you can use it in place of water for even more flavor.

6 chicken drumsticks (about 4 ounces each)

12 ounces napa cabbage

2 medium carrots

8 shiitake mushrooms, stems removed

One 14-ounce package firm tofu, drained and cut into 1-inch cubes

½ recipe Chicken Meatballs (Tsukune, page 182); uncooked and unsauced

FOR SERVING

Sea salt

Ponzu sauce

1. Put the chicken in a large (3- to 5-quart) nabe, Dutch oven, or braiser and cover with 8 cups water. Bring to a simmer over medium heat, skimming any ugly gray foam that floats to the surface, then reduce the heat to low, cover, and simmer for 20 minutes.

2. Meanwhile, prep the vegetables: Core the cabbage and slice it into 2-inch pieces. Peel the carrots and slice on the bias into ½-inch-thick ovals.

3. Add the cabbage, carrots, and mushrooms to the pot, cover, and cook until the vegetables begin to soften, about 8 minutes. Add the tofu and meatballs and simmer for 6 to 7 more minutes, or until the meatballs are cooked through.

4. Take the whole pot out to the table and let everyone pluck out what they want to eat. Tell them to try seasoning the meat and vegetables simply with sea salt first, before going for the ponzu. When you're finished, don't throw away the leftover broth! Use it to make Rice Porridge (Ojiya, page 114), or simply add some cooked noodles or a raw egg to turn it into a second meal.

Salmon and Miso Hot Pot (Ishikari Nabe)

Serves 4

My wife's family is from Hokkaido prefecture, home to the city of Ishikari, where this hot pot of salmon, pork belly, and vegetables comes from. When Mari and I got married and moved back to Japan from New York, this was one of the first things she asked me to cook for her. I had never had it before, so I went out and bought the ingredients, and she directed me in cooking them. She tasted it and said, "Oh my god, that's exactly right."

This is how our marriage works. I love Japan and Japanese food, but no matter how much time and energy I spend studying and learning, she'll always be ahead of me. There's no substitute for growing up living and breathing this stuff. Mari's been introducing me to new things for years, guiding me in how they should be made and how they should taste. Truth be told, she uses me like I'm a kitchen tool. I'm happy to oblige.

One 5-inch square kombu or
   4½ cups Dashi (page 28)
One 1-pound skin-on salmon fillet
2 carrots, peeled
1 large red potato, peeled
12 ounces napa cabbage
8 shiitake mushrooms, stems
   removed
10 ounces thinly sliced skinless
   pork belly (see Thinly Sliced Meat,
   page 129) or uncured bacon, cut
   into 1-inch pieces
One 14-ounce package soft tofu,
   drained and cut into 1-inch cubes
½ cup white (shiro) miso
¼ cup soy sauce
2 tablespoons sake
2 tablespoons mirin
3 tablespoons unsalted butter,
   cut into small cubes

FOR SERVING
Sea salt

1. Combine the kombu and 5 cups cold water in a large (3- to 5-quart) nabe, Dutch oven, or braiser and let the seaweed soak for at least 30 minutes or up to 1 hour. Or, if you have 4½ cups dashi at the ready, skip ahead to step 2.

2. Meanwhile, prep the fish, pork, and vegetables: Cut the salmon into 2-inch chunks. Slice the carrots on the bias into ½-inch-thick ovals. Cut the potato into 1-inch chunks. Core the cabbage and slice into 2-inch pieces.

3. Bring the water and kombu, if using, to a gentle simmer over medium heat and cook for 10 minutes, then remove the kombu. (Or simply bring the dashi to a simmer.) Add the carrots, potato, and shiitake mushrooms, cover, and cook

for 5 minutes, or until they begin to soften. Add the cabbage, cover again, and simmer for 3 to 4 more minutes, until the cabbage is wilted.

4. Add the salmon, pork, and tofu to the pot, cover, and simmer for 4 to 5 minutes, or until all the vegetables are tender and the salmon and pork are just cooked through.

5. Combine the miso, soy sauce, sake, and mirin in a bowl and add a ladleful of the broth from the pot, whisking to dissolve the miso. (This prevents lumps of miso in the broth.) Stir the mixture into the pot, turn off the heat, add the butter, and stir once more. Serve family-style, with a little bowl of sea salt on the side for people to season to taste.

Oyster and Cabbage Hot Pot (Kaki Nabe)

Serves 4

I think oysters are one of the world's few perfect foods. They're the embodiment of freshness, and they give off the impression of luxury without being decadent. Obviously, if you don't feel the same way about oysters, this isn't the recipe for you. Actually, if you don't love oysters, I'm not sure we can be friends.

This dish, like Every-Night Hot Pot (Jouya Nabe, page 132), is incredibly light and subtle. It needs a splash of soy sauce and citrus for seasoning, and then perhaps a bowl of rice or Grilled Rice Balls (Yaki Onigiri, page 186) on the side to make it a full meal. But if you throw in a glass of sparkling wine, you have yourself a sophisticated, elegant supper with little effort.

One 5-inch square kombu or 6 cups Dashi (page 28)

12 ounces napa cabbage, cored and sliced into 3-inch pieces

6 shiitake mushrooms, stems removed and caps quartered

One 14-ounce package soft tofu, cut into 2-inch cubes

6 very fresh large oysters (7 to 8 ounces total), sliced into 1-inch chunks

FOR SERVING

Ginger-Onion Shio Tare (page 181)

Soy sauce

Citrus wedges (lime, lemon, Meyer lemon, or yuzu)

1. Combine the kombu and 6½ cups cold water in a large (3- to 5-quart) nabe, Dutch oven, or braiser and let the seaweed soak for 30 minutes to 1 hour. Or, if you have 6 cups dashi at the ready, skip ahead to step 2.

2. Bring the water to a simmer over medium-high heat, then fish the kombu out of the pot. (Or simply bring the dashi to a simmer). Add the cabbage and mushrooms, drop the heat to low, and cook until the cabbage is tender, about 6 minutes. Add the tofu and cook for 3 minutes, or until it's warmed through. Stir in the oysters and simmer until they're barely cooked through, about 3 minutes. Serve family-style, with the sauces and citrus wedges on the side for dipping and seasoning.

Beef Hot Pot (Sukiyaki)

Serves 4

While sushi has become the emblematic Japanese food for most Americans, it actually wasn't until the eighties that we became infatuated—or even comfortable—with the idea of raw fish. For much of the preceding eighty or ninety years, Americans traveling to Japan or dining in Japanese-American restaurants were looking for one thing: a bubbling pot of beef, vegetables, and noodles in soy-flavored broth. They were looking for sukiyaki.

To my mind, sukiyaki makes the best case for the delights of thinly sliced beef. It's also my favorite way of eating premium-quality meat. On the rare occasion that I spring for some high-end Wagyu beef, we always cook it in sukiyaki. After a brief swim in sweet-salty broth, the beef is meltingly tender and perfectly seasoned. With a quick dip in egg yolk, it's the perfect bite of food.

12 ounces (2 packages) shirataki noodles or fresh ramen noodles

½ cup soy sauce

½ cup sake

½ cup mirin

¼ cup sugar

2 tablespoons vegetable oil

1 bunch scallions, cut into 2-inch lengths

8 ounces napa cabbage, cored and cut into 2-inch pieces

About 5 ounces (1 package) enoki mushrooms, trimmed

One 14-ounce package medium or firm tofu, drained and cut into 1-inch cubes

About 5 ounces chrysanthemum greens or dandelion greens

1½ pounds thinly sliced beef (preferably rib-eye or another tender cut; see Thinly Sliced Meat, page 129)

GARNISHES

4 raw egg yolks (of a quality and freshness you feel comfortable eating raw)

Steamed rice (page 25)

1. If using shirataki noodles, bring 2 cups water to a boil in a small saucepan. Meanwhile, place the shirataki noodles in a colander in the sink and rinse with cold water. Pour the boiling water over the noodles to help remove any funky odor.

2. Whisk together the soy sauce, sake, mirin, sugar, and 2¼ cups water in a bowl, stirring to dissolve the sugar. Set aside.

3. Heat a large (3- to 5-quart) nabe, Dutch oven, or braiser over medium heat, then coat with the vegetable oil. (If you own a portable gas or electric stove, do this tableside and keep the pot simmering throughout dinner.) Add the scallions and sauté until softened and slightly wilted, about 3 minutes. Add the cabbage, mushrooms, tofu, and shirataki noodles (or fresh ramen). If your pot isn't large enough to accommodate all the ingredients at once, start with

half and add the rest when you've finished the first batch. Pour the soy sauce mixture over everything, cover the pot, and simmer for 10 minutes, or until the vegetables are nearly cooked through.

4. With the sauce simmering, pile the chrysanthemum greens on top of everything, cover, and simmer over low heat for a couple minutes, or until the greens are just wilted. Finally, start adding the beef a little bit at a time. Drag each slice through the sauce before tucking it into a corner of the pot to simmer until the meat reaches your desired level of doneness.

5. Give each diner his or her own little soup bowl with an egg yolk cracked into it and a bowl of rice on the side. Serve the sukiyaki family-style, so everyone can pluck out what they like, dip it in egg, and eat it with rice.

Otaku
(Geeking Out)

The Specialists

As a cook, like most of my American colleagues, I've always been inspired by Japanese cooks and their commitment to perfecting their specialty. It's what drove me to open Ivan Ramen. From the moment I set foot in Japan, I found myself surrounded by people who had dedicated themselves to doing one thing really well, whether it was the vendor who made a specific kind of mochi cake all day every day, the carpenter who built whole houses without using a single nail, or the kintsugi specialist who painstakingly repaired broken ceramics with lacquer and gold. Japanese speakers refer to these hyperfocused experts as *shokunin*. I wanted to know more; I wanted to be that good at something myself.

Of course, achieving mastery requires single-minded devotion to one's craft. Over the next decade and a half of living off and on in Tokyo, I was occupied with meeting my first wife, attending culinary school in New York, having my first son, mourning my first wife's death, meeting my new wife and her son, and then moving back to Japan on a long-term basis. Finally, in the late nineties, I caught the ramen bug. I began obsessively eating as much ramen as I could, just as more and more shops in town were beginning to serve nuanced, thoughtful bowls. And for a while, that's as far as it went: I was a fan.

However, after I lollygagged around for a few years while Mari brought home the bacon, a combination of restlessness and free time pushed me to do something more with ramen. Twenty years after my first trip to the country, I combined my Western cooking education with my passion for Japanese noodles and opened my first ramen shop in Tokyo. I'll tell you what, there are very few things that can acclimate you to life in a foreign country more fully than opening a business there.

I'm not trying to toot my own horn too hard, but making it in the Japanese restaurant scene isn't easy for an outsider. You can't just walk into a

sushi shop and ask for a job slicing fish. Ramen's a little more open-minded, but breaking through took patience and not a small amount of guts. Japanese diners are sophisticated. Ramen eaters are persnickety. If I hadn't taken the craft seriously, they would have burned me alive. Pulling it off while helping to raise three young sons didn't make it any easier, but I think it proves that you can have kids and still chase new dreams. It starts with finding the intersection of your existing skills and interests. From there it's a matter of diving into the deep end.

All that being said, I'm still loath to consider myself a shokunin. I think of myself more like an *otaku*—a geek. The term is broad and covers a range of hard-core fans, from anime fiends to gamers to foodies. If shokunin is the idealized vision of Japanese people as master artisans, otaku is the stereotype of Japanese fetishists. The truth, I think, is that they're two branches of the same tree. For my part, I was something like a ramen otaku who parlayed my fascination with soup into a studious practice.

A common refrain among American chefs who have spent time studying Japanese cuisine is that Western cooks lack the devotion to doing one thing well. There are no good cooks, they say, because everybody suffers from occupational ADHD. One week they want to make sushi, the next week pizza,

Top: The sushi master at Fujisei in Azabujuban.
Bottom left: A beef croquette (menchi katsu) from Niku no Ohyama.
Bottom right: Handmade gyoza, a labor of love.

and a month later they want to be food writers. I'm not so bold as to make a sweeping generalization like that, but I do think we could all benefit from experiencing the satisfaction and rewards of geeking out on something.

In this chapter, I set out to translate otaku into a few recipes that, I hope, will demonstrate the upside of otaku. None of them require you to be exceptionally skilled as a cook, but they all require a little more effort, attention, and time than the other recipes in this book. This is project cooking—things you have to set aside the time and energy for. In the case of the Oden Party (page 146), that means putting in a little more effort on the shopping side. With Chicken Dan Dan Noodles (page 150), it's more about patience: You're going to have to spend one day making soup and another day preparing the toppings before you get to eat. And in the subsection in the latter part of the chapter, I'm encouraging you to take frying more seriously. It's not just the domain of fast-food restaurants. There's an art to monitoring hot oil (and being willing to clean up afterward). I'm betting you find it's all worth the trouble.

Opposite: A vendor at a local fair makes mochi cakes stuffed with pork and vegetables.
Above: Chefs working the line at the kaiseki restaurant Shokuzen Abe in Ginza.

Oden Party

Serves 4 to 6

In the winter months in Tokyo, I used to visit a *yatai*—a mobile food stall—that sold oden in the Koenji neighborhood. There wasn't much to the place beyond a little roof, with a plastic screen to protect diners from the cold. I'd take a seat, and the vendor, who looked like he was pushing 150 years old, would dip an aluminum cup into hot water to heat it up, then fill it with hot sake for me. I'd sit there clutching my cup for warmth, choosing whatever fish cakes and vegetables I wanted from a big steaming basin of dashi. The vendor would retrieve the items one by one with a pair of long chopsticks and serve them to me. This all took place thirty years ago, but those oden meals remain among my strongest food memories.

These days oden is usually confined to convenience stores in Japan. But if you do find a really great oden restaurant, it's a transcendent experience. There will be a half-dozen varieties of homemade fish cakes, things done with tofu that you'd never imagine, cabbage stuffed with yuba (tofu skin), foods tied into neat packages with kelp and strings of dried gourd (*kanpyo*), and daikon, beef tongue, beef tendon, octopus, even whale. Everything is cooked perfectly, often in its own batch of dashi. It's tremendous fun to eat, and satisfying but not heavy.

At home I don't get quite so ambitious. I like to simmer a big pot of dashi seasoned with soy sauce, sake, and mirin and add items in the order of their cooking times. I definitely don't make my own fish cakes either, so I'm giving you complete permission to rely heavily on packaged food here. Go to a Japanese or Korean market and stock up on fish balls, fish cakes, and various types of tofu. Add some daikon and eggs, cook everything to its ideal doneness, and bring it out to the table. If you have a portable burner or an induction cooker, set it on low and set the pot on top. Give everyone a plate and serve them one or two pieces at a time with sides of karashi (Japanese mustard) and sliced negi (Japanese green onions) or scallions.

BROTH

8 cups Dashi (page 28)

3 tablespoons soy sauce

3 tablespoons sake

3 tablespoons mirin

PACKAGED INGREDIENTS

Choose three or four.

12 ounces (2 packages) shirataki noodles

Chikuwa (cylindrical fish cakes), left whole

Satsuma-age (fried fish cakes), left whole

Abura-age (fried tofu)

Hanpen (white fish cakes), cut into triangles or smaller squares

Japanese (arabiki) sausages (or hot dogs or Vienna sausages)

Kombu maki (dried seaweed rolls), soaked in hot water for 5 minutes

FRESH INGREDIENTS

Daikon is a must. Eggs are optional.

12 ounces daikon, peeled and sliced into ½-inch-thick rounds

4 large eggs or Soy-Marinated Eggs (Ajitama, page 30; optional)

FOR SERVING

Spicy Japanese mustard (karashi)

Thinly sliced negi (Japanese green onions) or scallions, sprinkled with sansho pepper

1. **FOR THE BROTH:** Add the dashi, soy sauce, sake, and mirin to a large pot or Dutch oven set over medium heat and bring to a bare simmer. Meanwhile, if using shirataki noodles, rinse them in a colander in the sink with cold water, then pour 2 cups boiling water over them to help remove any funky odor.

2. Begin adding ingredients to the simmering broth in the order of their cooking times, longer-cooking items first—see the chart on pages 148 and 149. Keep the heat at a bare simmer and work in batches if necessary. With the exception of the daikon and eggs, you're not trying to cook anything, per se. You're mostly reheating and infusing dashi flavor into precooked foods.

3. Distribute bowls and serve people one or two pieces at a time with a splash of broth, a smear of mustard, and a handful of green onions on the side.

Oden Ingredient Cooking Times

Abura-age
5 minutes

Shirataki noodles
10 minutes

Hanpen
5 minutes

Japanese sausages
(or hot dogs or Vienna sausages)
10 minutes

Chikuwa
5 minutes

Satsuma-age
5 minutes

Eggs
15 minutes;
peel, then return
to the pot for
5 to 10 minutes

Daikon
40 to 50 minutes

Kombu maki
10 minutes

Chicken Dan Dan Noodles

Serves 4

Dan dan noodles are actually a Chinese dish, but they're a mainstay of the Ivan Ramen menu. I'm kind of obsessed with them. I love how dynamic the flavor is—a constant push and pull between fat and acid, sweet and salty, spicy heat and numbing Sichuan peppercorns. The dish has endless variations. It can be soupy or dry, rich with peanut butter or sesame paste, spicy or mild; made with pork or chicken; and often bursting with the tartness of pickled mustard greens. We've done many versions of dan dan at the restaurants over the years, but this is the one I keep coming back to.

I've filed this recipe as an Otaku dish, partly because it's a product of my own personal fixation, but also because it takes a bit more work than most other recipes in the book. Nothing fancy or complicated, but some careful shopping and slow cooking are required. You use a whole chicken to make the broth. (There will be too much broth, but there's no way to make a smaller batch. Plus, it's chicken broth—I'm sure you'll find a way to use it.) You're going to need to find shiro shoyu (white soy sauce) at an Asian market or online. You also need to find brown rice vinegar, most likely at a boutique grocery store. And you're going to need to locate fresh noodles that you like, whether that means ramen, Chinese soup noodles, or Italian pasta.

The recipe is divided into three parts: the broth, the tare (seasoning sauce), and the chicken topping. You can make the first two components in advance, then warm up the soup once you're ready to serve the noodles.

BROTH

1 whole chicken (about 4 pounds), preferably with head and feet still attached

2 pounds chicken feet or 3 pounds chicken backs

TARE (SEASONING SAUCE)

1 teaspoon Sichuan peppercorns

1 teaspoon red pepper flakes

2 tablespoons toasted sesame oil

2 tablespoons chicken fat, reserved from the broth (or vegetable oil)

2 tablespoons finely sliced scallions

¼ cup white soy sauce (shiro shoyu; see headnote)

2 tablespoons brown rice vinegar (see headnote; use regular rice vinegar in a pinch)

½ teaspoon sugar

½ teaspoon kosher salt

CHICKEN TOPPING

1 tablespoon Sichuan peppercorns

1 tablespoon red pepper flakes

2 tablespoons toasted sesame oil

3 tablespoons chicken fat, reserved from the broth (or vegetable oil)

3 tablespoons chopped scallion whites

1 tablespoon minced or grated ginger

1 tablespoon minced garlic

¼ cup sesame seeds

1 pound ground chicken

2 tablespoons sugar

2 teaspoons kosher salt

FOR SERVING

1 pound fresh ramen noodles or any thick fresh noodle you like

Chopped scallions

1. **FOR THE BROTH:** Place the whole chicken in a large stockpot. Add the chicken feet or backs and cover with 5 quarts cold water. Bring to a simmer over medium heat, skimming any gray scum that floats to the surface during the first 10 to 15 minutes of cooking. Reduce the heat to medium-low and simmer for 6 hours, replenishing the broth with fresh water as it reduces. (I like to mark the top

RECIPE CONTINUES

of the water line with a permanent marker at the beginning, so I don't forget where I started.) Strain the broth, let cool to room temperature, and refrigerate overnight.

2. The next day, scrape the fat off the top of the broth and reserve 5 tablespoons separately. (You will only need 2 cups broth for this recipe, but you can easily freeze the leftovers and use them wherever a clean, flavorful chicken stock will come in handy.)

3. **FOR THE TARE:** Grind the Sichuan peppercorns and red pepper flakes together in a spice grinder; set aside. Heat a small skillet over medium heat, then add the sesame oil and the 2 tablespoons reserved chicken fat (or vegetable oil). Add the ground spices and sliced scallions and cook, stirring

constantly, until the scallions have wilted slightly and the spices are very fragrant, about 2 minutes. Remove from the heat and immediately stir in the white soy sauce, vinegar, sugar, and salt. Transfer to a large bowl.

4. Bring a large pot of water to a boil for the noodles and season liberally with salt. In a separate saucepan, reheat 2 cups chicken broth over low heat.

5. **MEANWHILE, FOR THE CHICKEN TOPPING:** Grind the Sichuan peppercorns and red pepper flakes together in a spice grinder; set aside. Heat a large skillet over medium heat, then coat with the sesame oil and the 3 tablespoons reserved chicken fat. Add the scallions, ginger, and garlic and cook until very fragrant, about 2 minutes. Stir in

the ground spices and sesame seeds and cook for another 2 minutes. Add the ground chicken, sugar, and salt and sauté, using a fork or wooden spoon to break up the chicken, until the meat is cooked through and any liquid has mostly cooked off, about 5 minutes.

6. Once the chicken is ready, drop the noodles into the boiling water and cook until al dente. Drain the noodles thoroughly in a colander, shaking them to remove the excess water.

7. To serve, whisk the hot broth into the reserved tare. Add the cooked noodles and toss to combine thoroughly. Portion among four bowls and top each with a quarter of the chicken topping. Garnish with chopped scallions and serve immediately.

Gyoza

Makes about 60 gyoza (enough to serve 4 or 5 hungry people)

There is no greater harbinger of joy than a big platter of dumplings. One of my best and earliest memories of Asia was landing in Taiwan for the first time and going out with friends to a restaurant where we demolished tray after tray of steamed and panfried dumplings, accompanied by glass after frosty glass of ice-cold beer.

In Japan, gyoza are the preeminent dumpling: filled with pork, crisp and brown on the bottom, chewy on top. I can polish off a dozen on my own without blinking. We've made gyoza on innumerable occasions at our house, experimenting with a different recipe each time. Unless you're a real putz, homemade gyoza are almost always better than store-bought ones. This is our best version—a product of a lot of trial and error and hundreds of gyozas eaten in the name of research. I'm counting gyoza as otaku because of the effort that went into developing my ideal version and the manual labor that goes into folding them.

One bonus feature I'm including here that we don't always do at home is the crisp "net" that a lot of gyoza shops serve with their dumplings. It's not that difficult to pull off, provided you have a good nonstick pan: You pour a little flour-water mixture into the pan as the gyoza cook and then invert the whole thing onto a plate to reveal a paper-thin wafer connecting all the gyoza. It takes some practice, but I'm willing to bet that by the time you finish cooking all sixty gyoza, you will have gotten it right at least once. Or just omit it entirely—it's totally optional.

---

1 pound green cabbage

1 tablespoon plus 1 teaspoon kosher salt

12 ounces ground pork

1 tablespoon plus 1 teaspoon minced or grated ginger

1 tablespoon plus 1 teaspoon minced garlic

1 cup garlic chives (nira) or regular chives, cut into ¼-inch pieces

1 tablespoon soy sauce

1 tablespoon toasted sesame oil

60 gyoza wrappers (as thin as you can find)

Cornstarch or potato starch for sprinkling

LATTICE NET (OPTIONAL)

All-purpose flour

FOR SERVING

Gyoza Dipping Sauce (page 155)

1. Chop the cabbage (or process in a food processor) into confetti-size bits and place in a colander or sieve. Toss with 2 teaspoons of the salt and let sit for 20 minutes in the sink. Gently press the cabbage to squeeze out as much water as you can.

2. Combine the drained cabbage, pork, ginger, garlic, chives, soy sauce, sesame oil, and the remaining 2 teaspoons salt in a large bowl and mix thoroughly so that everything is evenly distributed, but don't overdo it. Too much handling

and the fat in the pork will begin to melt.

3. Here's where you want to employ some extra hands to help you. Have your filling and wrappers near at hand. Fill a small bowl with water and sprinkle a baking sheet with cornstarch or potato starch to receive the finished dumplings. For each gyoza, place a wrapper in the palm of your hand and spoon about 1½ teaspoons filling onto the center. Use the back of the spoon to smoosh it lightly. You don't want the filling to run to the edges, but you also don't want it sitting in a fat clump in the middle. Dip your

RECIPE CONTINUES

finger in the bowl of water and run it along the perimeter of one half of the wrapper. Now you're going to fold the wet edge of the wrapper over to meet the dry edge, but you also want those nice signature gyoza pleats: Start by crimping the edges together at one corner, then proceed around the dumpling, using your finger to push the dough into little pleats on one side and pressing them against the other side to seal it. (If that's difficult for you to visualize, this is what the internet was made for. There are hundreds of gyoza-folding videos out there you can refer to.) Place the dumplings on the tray as you finish them and sprinkle with starch to prevent sticking.

4. To cook the gyoza, you will need a 10-inch nonstick pan or an incredibly well-seasoned carbon steel pan (otherwise, they will really stick), either one with a lid. Arrange 10 to 15 gyoza in a circle in the pan and set over medium heat. Add enough water to come a quarter of the way up the sides of the gyoza, cover, and let the water cook away, about 5 minutes.

5. **MEANWHILE, IF YOU WANT TO MAKE THE LATTICE NET:** Whisk together 1 teaspoon flour with 5 tablespoons water in a bowl.

6. Once the water has evaporated from the pan, remove the lid and add the lattice batter, if using. Swirl the pan to distribute the batter evenly and cook until the batter has browned, about 3 minutes. If you don't want the

lattice, simply continue to cook until the bottoms of the gyoza are browned. If you make the net, remove the pan from the heat and, while holding a plate on top of the gyoza, flip the pan over and give it a good downward shake. This should dislodge the gyoza and lattice net onto the plate. If the net sticks or falls apart, don't despair. The dumplings will still be delicious, and you'll have another shot at it the next time around. Serve with the dipping sauce.

NOTE: Uncooked gyoza can be frozen on a baking sheet in a single layer until firm and then stored in zip-top bags for a couple months.

To cook frozen gyoza, add a second batch of water in step 4 after the first batch evaporates.

Gyoza Dipping Sauce
Makes a generous ¼ cup

¼ **cup soy sauce**
1 **tablespoon plus 1 teaspoon rice vinegar**
1 **teaspoon Japanese chili oil (rayu) or Chunky Chili Oil (page 234)**

Mix everything together in a small bowl. Serve in dipping saucers with the gyoza. If your guests like things a little spicier, set out more chili oil to add to taste.

FRYING

Frying gets a bad rap, and I can understand why. In America, fried food is the stuff of county fairs and McDonald's. It's greasy and junky. The act of frying is generally regarded as a technique that requires so little skill that they let stoned teenagers do it. Everything gets tossed into a vat of hot oil and comes out crisp and halfway decent tasting. It's hard to fuck up that badly, especially because people tend to be forgiving when it comes to fried food. We don't even really seem to mind when the fryer oil is old and reused and the beignets taste like fish sticks.

But a lifetime of eating in Japan has shown me that frying can actually be super-elegant. You can bathe a steak in hot oil to achieve a perfectly rare center and a crisp exterior. You can gently coat seasonal vegetables and herbs in brittle jackets of cake flour batter. And you can make lowbrow food really majestic too. Fried Shrimp (Ebi Fry, page 169) and Beef Croquettes (Menchi Katsu, page 166) are some of the greatest guilty-pleasure treats on the planet.

I consider frying an otaku cooking technique for two reasons: First, it really does take a certain amount of finesse to fry properly. You need to dial in your batter or coating so that it doesn't fall off or cake into a thick mass in the oil. You have to keep a careful eye on the oil temperature. Timing is critical too, as is frequent skimming, to prevent any leftover bits from burning and tainting the oil. Second, frying is really an ordeal that only devout fried-food lovers will pursue. You have to buy a bunch of oil. You have to figure out where to dispose of that oil when you're done. You have to scrub your kitchen down to remove the film of oil that will cover everything. And, unless you have an industrial-strength exhaust fan, you have to live in a house that smells like fried food for a day or two.

Tempura Party

Serves 4

In Japan, tempura can be a thing of beauty. Not all the time, obviously—there's plenty of low-end tempura in Japan—but at its zenith, Japanese tempura is unlike anything I've had in the States. The really great tempura restaurants treat tempura like sushi. They make and serve one piece at a time, using only the freshest seasonal vegetables, herbs, and seafood. The batter is exquisitely light, a thin and delicate shell clinging to what's inside, never greasy or soggy.

I'm not expecting you to rise to the same level of oneness with hot oil as Japanese chefs, but when you make tempura at home, you can take some hints from the best. Begin by choosing ingredients that are in season and at their peak. Think outside the box of what you've had at restaurants. Unexpected things like chrysanthemum greens are shockingly delicious when battered and fried. Listed below are some suggestions that will be widely available, but you should try anything interesting you come upon at the farmers' market.

Next, don't try to make an elaborate combination tempura platter. Serve one item at a time and concentrate on getting it right. Use a deep-frying oil thermometer and keep an eye on it. People tend to get lazy when they fry. Maybe you start with your oil at 350°F, but then you overload the pot and the temp drops to 225°F, so your food gets a nice soak in warm oil. Or maybe you leave the heat too high, so the oil creeps up to 450°F, and everything takes on the flavor of burnt oil. All of this is why I consider tempura to be an otaku thing—it takes care and attention. It's also a bit difficult to pull off for more than four people at a time.

You can serve the tempura simply with dipping sauce or with steamed rice and Ten Don Sauce (page 161)—the same sweet-salty topping used to top Shrimp-Vegetable Fritter Rice Bowl (Kakiage Don, page 162).

FIRM VEGETABLES
Choose a couple.

Carrots, peeled and cut on the bias into ¼-inch-thick slices
Lotus root, peeled and sliced into ¼-inch-thick rounds
Kabocha squash, quartered, seeded, and sliced into ¼-inch-thick crescents
Sweet potato, peeled and sliced into ¼-inch-thick rounds
Onion, peeled and sliced into ½-inch-thick rounds and separated into rings

SOFT VEGETABLES
Choose a couple.

Maitake, shimeji (beech), or oyster mushrooms, trimmed and torn into finger-size chunks
Shiitake mushrooms, stems removed
Asparagus, woody bottoms removed, peeled, and sliced in half
Chrysanthemum or dandelion greens, torn into 2-inch pieces
Okra (whole)
Zucchini, sliced on the bias into ½-inch-thick pieces

SEAFOOD

Medium or large shrimp, peeled but tail left on (give the back of each shrimp a couple light whacks against a cutting board to break up the muscle fibers and prevent them from curling as they cook)
Squid bodies, sliced into rings

4 to 6 quarts vegetable oil for deep-frying

RECIPE CONTINUES

BATTER

If you want more batter than this, make it in batches. Don't try to double or triple the recipe. This batter is extremely light—not like what you'll find at most Japanese-American restaurants. It will give the seafood and vegetables a gossamer-thin coating of crunchiness.

2 large egg yolks
1¼ cups cake flour, sifted

FOR SERVING

Tempura Dipping Sauce
   (recipe follows)
Ten Don Sauce (recipe follows;
   optional)
Steamed rice (page 25; optional)

1. Have the vegetables and/or seafood at the ready. Add the vegetable oil to an 8- to 10-quart heavy-bottomed pot. (If you have a deep fryer, more power to you.) Heat the oil to 350°F over medium heat, using a deep-fry thermometer to check the temperature. Line a baking sheet with paper towels or a wire rack to receive the fried items.

2. **FOR THE BATTER:** It's important that the water be very cold, so begin by making a couple cups of ice water, then straining and measuring out 1¾ cups. Pour the water into a bowl, add the egg yolks, and whisk thoroughly to combine. Add the flour and whisk very lightly. Resist the urge to overmix—it's fine if a few lumps remain—and you will be rewarded with an airy, lattice-like tempura.

3. Meanwhile, set your guests up with individual bowls of sauce(s) and rice, if you're serving it.

4. Once the oil is hot, start with whichever ingredient you like. Give it a quick dip into the batter, using your fingers or wooden chopsticks, then give it a little shake to let any excess drip back into the bowl. Lower the battered ingredient into the oil and give it a gentle stir. Most items will take somewhere around 90 seconds to cook through and crisp up, but you'll want to test a piece of each one to get the timing right first. Never fry so many items simultaneously that the oil temperature drops dramatically. Remove the fried items from the oil and let drain for a few seconds, then serve while still hot and crisp.

Tempura Dipping Sauce

Makes 1½ cups

1 cup Dashi (page 28)
¼ cup soy sauce
¼ cup mirin
½ cup finely grated daikon

Combine the dashi, soy sauce, and mirin in a bowl, then divide among individual dipping bowls. Set out the grated daikon in a separate bowl so diners can add a couple tablespoons or so to taste.

Ten Don Sauce

Makes 1½ cups

4 cups Dashi (page 28)
¾ cup soy sauce
½ cup mirin
2 tablespoons sugar

Combine the dashi, soy sauce, mirin, and sugar in a saucepan and bring to a simmer over medium heat, stirring to dissolve the sugar. Cook until the liquid is reduced by about 75 percent and the sauce is syrupy, about 9 minutes. Cool and store in the fridge for up to a week. Serve cool or at room temperature.

Shrimp-Vegetable Fritter Rice Bowl (Kakiage Don)

Serves 4

I've noticed that many people who are otherwise perfectly reasonable will draw an irrational line in the sand when it comes to eating carbs on top of other carbs. Is it some kind of post-Atkins-trauma thing?

Kakiage—a fritter of shrimp and shredded vegetables—can be eaten on its own, but it's really better on top of rice. You'll just have to come to terms with eating fried food on a bed of starch. Kakiage can include whatever seasonal vegetables you want, but it's best if you choose ingredients that will all cook in the same amount of time.

4 to 6 quarts vegetable oil for deep-frying

8 ounces shrimp, peeled and cut into ½-inch chunks

2 carrots, peeled and cut into matchsticks

1 onion, sliced thin

4 stalks asparagus, woody bottoms removed, quartered lengthwise, and sliced into matchsticks

1 ear corn, husked and kernels sliced off

Tempura Batter (page 161)

FOR SERVING

Steamed rice (page 25)

Ten Don Sauce (page 161)

1. Heat 3 to 4 inches of oil to 350°F in a large (8- to 10-quart) pot over medium heat. Line a baking sheet with paper towels or a wire rack.

2. Toss together the shrimp, carrots, onion, asparagus, and corn in a bowl. Scoop ¼ cup of the vegetable mixture into the tempura batter, then use a slotted spoon to scoop up the mix, shake off some of the excess batter, and gently lower the mixture into the hot oil. Cook for about 1 minute; the batter should bind the mixture into a rough disk. Flip the disk over and cook for another minute, or until both sides are crisp and very lightly browned. Transfer to the paper towels or wire rack to drain. Repeat with the remaining shrimp-and-vegetable mixture.

3. Serve over steamed rice with a heavy drizzle of ten don sauce.

Chicken-Fried Steak with Wasabi-Joyu (Gyukatsu)

Serves 4

When it comes to breaded-and-fried meat, for many years it seemed like there was only Tonkatsu (Fried Pork Cutlets, page 44). But in recent days, gyukatsu—panko-crusted beef—has taken off in Japan. In parts of Kansai (southern Japan), it's even more popular than tonkatsu.

The hallmark of a good gyukatsu is a crunchy-crisp exterior and a ruby-red rare interior. The secret is a thick piece of meat that you don't fry straight out of the fridge. Let the steak sit at room temperature for half an hour before cooking. The sauce for gyukatsu is wasabi-joyu, which is simply your favorite soy sauce mixed with the best wasabi you can find. (Bet you didn't know there was a name for this.) If you love wasabi, add more; if you're sensitive, dial it back. And, as with sushi, you don't want to drown the meat in sauce—a quick dip of one corner of each bite is plenty.

One 1-pound boneless rib-eye steak (about 1 inch thick), left to rest at room temperature for 30 minutes
¼ cup all-purpose flour
1 large egg
1 cup panko, plus more as needed
Vegetable oil for shallow-frying

FOR SERVING
Wasabi paste (the stuff from a tube is fine)
Soy sauce
Thinly sliced cabbage

1. Trim off any big chunks of fat from the steak, then cut the steak on the bias against the grain, into 4 thick pieces. Working with one piece at a time, place each piece on a cutting board and cover it with a piece of plastic wrap. Use a rolling pin or empty wine bottle to pound it lightly to a uniform thickness of about ¾ inch.

2. Set up a breading station by lining up three shallow trays—pie tins work well—and filling them with the flour, egg, and panko, respectively. Lightly beat the egg. Bread the cutlets one at a time, first coating in flour, shaking off the excess, then dipping into the egg, and, finally, coating with bread crumbs, using your fingers to press the panko onto the surface of the cutlets. Set aside on a plate.

3. Fill a deep heavy-bottomed skillet with ⅓ inch of oil and heat the oil over medium heat to 375°F. (As a rough guide, you can tell if the oil is ready by tossing a pinch of panko into the pan. If it sizzles and browns quickly, it's hot enough.) Line a baking sheet with paper towels or a wire rack.

4. Fry the cutlets in batches until the exterior is crisp and browned but the meat is still rare, about 30 seconds per side. Transfer the cooked cutlets to the paper towels or wire rack to rest and drain for a few minutes.

5. For each diner, mix together ½ teaspoon wasabi (or to taste) and 1 tablespoon soy sauce in a sauce ramekin. Slice the cutlets into thick pieces and serve with the sauce and a pile of freshly sliced cabbage.

Beef Croquettes (Menchi Katsu)

Makes 8 croquettes (enough to serve 4 with leftovers for sandwiches)

Menchi katsu is a less well known but no less delicious cousin of Tonkatsu (page 44) and Gyukatsu (page 165), although it's really closer in composition to a croquette (*korokke*). Picture a blend of ground beef and vegetables formed into a puck, coated with panko, and fried until crisp.

Hot out of the fryer, menchi katsu are terrific drinking snacks, but don't sleep on menchi katsu sandwiches. Use fresh patties or reheat leftover ones in a toaster oven and stuff them between slices of white bread (see page 103) slathered in Kewpie mayo and Bull-Dog tonkatsu sauce. This recipe yields more menchi katsu than four people can eat in one sitting, because I know you'll want to eat them again the next day.

8 ounces green cabbage, cored and shredded (about 1¾ cups)

Kosher salt

1¼ pounds ground beef (the fattier the better)

1 large onion, finely diced

3 large eggs

1 tablespoon oyster sauce

1 tablespoon ketchup

1 tablespoon Bull-Dog tonkatsu sauce

2 cups panko

½ cup all-purpose flour

Vegetable oil for shallow-frying

FOR SERVING

Thinly sliced cabbage

Bull-Dog tonkatsu sauce

1. Place the cabbage in a colander and toss with 1 teaspoon salt. Let sit for 10 minutes in the sink to draw out some of the water.

2. Combine the ground beef, diced onion, 1 egg, the oyster sauce, ketchup, and Bull-Dog sauce in a bowl. Squeeze the water out of the salted cabbage as best you can and add it to the meat mixture, along with ½ cup of the panko and 1 teaspoon salt. Use clean hands to mix everything together thoroughly. Form the meat mixture into eight pucks, each about ¾ inch thick.

3. Set up a breading station by lining up three shallow trays—pie tins work well—and filling them with the flour, the remaining 2 eggs, and the rest of the panko, respectively. Lightly beat the eggs. Working with one at a time, coat each meat patty with flour, gently dusting off any excess, then give it a dip in egg, and, finally, a coating of panko. Don't be stingy with the bread crumbs—cover the whole

patty and press down gently to ensure they adhere. Set aside on a plate.

4. Fill a deep heavy-bottomed skillet with ⅓ inch of oil and heat the oil over medium heat to 325°F. (As a rough guide, you can tell if the oil is ready by tossing a pinch of panko into the pan. If it sizzles immediately, it's hot enough.) Line a baking sheet with paper towels or a wire rack to receive the fried menchi katsu.

5. Fry the menchi katsu in batches until they're deep golden brown, 3 to 4 minutes per side. (If the katsu are browning more quickly than that, your oil is too hot.) Season with salt as they come out of the pan and let them rest and drain for a couple minutes on the paper towels or wire rack.

6. Serve with a pile of thinly sliced cabbage and Bull-Dog sauce for dipping. Make sandwiches with the leftovers.

Fried Shrimp (Ebi Fry)

Serves 4 as an appetizer

A perfectly fried plump shrimp is unbeatable in my book. Kids and grown-ups love them equally, and there's really nothing complicated about making them. I'll sometimes buy 2 pounds of shrimp, fry them, and pile them up for my youngest son, Ren, who eats them in front of the TV like they're potato chips.

The shrimp for a classic ebi fry, a staple of yoshoku restaurants, are usually straightened out before frying, either via skewers or by scoring the backs of the shrimp and slapping them against a cutting board. You can use either method or choose to forgo the straightening process altogether.

8 large shrimp, peeled, tails left attached, and deveined

6 cups vegetable oil for deep-frying

⅓ cup all-purpose flour

1 large egg

½ cup panko

Kosher salt

FOR SERVING

Lemon wedges

Thinly sliced cabbage

Bull-Dog tonkatsu sauce and/or tartar sauce

1. If you want to straighten the shrimp before frying, you can do so in one of two ways: You can run a short bamboo skewer through the length of each shrimp, then remove it after frying. Or—this is my preferred method—you can make a few shallow incisions along the belly (inside curve) of each shrimp, grab it by the tail, and give its back a few gentle whacks against a cutting board to break up the muscle fibers. Place the shrimp on a paper towel to dry.

2. Add the vegetable oil to a deep 4-quart heavy-bottomed saucepan and heat the oil to 350°F over medium heat. Line a baking sheet with paper towels or a wire rack.

3. Meanwhile, set up a breading station by lining up three shallow trays—pie tins work well—and filling them with the flour, egg, and panko, respectively. Lightly beat the egg. Working with one at a time, coat each shrimp with flour, gently dusting off any excess, then give it a dip in egg, and, finally, a coating of panko. Set aside on a plate.

4. Fry the shrimp in batches for about 2 minutes, or until the exterior is crisp and golden brown. Drain on the paper towels or wire rack and season lightly with salt. Serve with lemon wedges, sliced cabbage, and whichever sauce(s) you prefer.

The ebi fry at Seiyoken in Asakusa is the platonic ideal of fried shrimp, so this is a photo of theirs, not ours. But don't worry, our recipe will produce very similar results.

Good
Times

The Fun Experts

Living in Japan, I watched with admiration as people elevated courtesy and craft to near-religious levels. Same with work ethic. But for an outsider like me who's not naturally inclined to be either polite or devout, the aspect of Japanese culture I latched on to most easily was their devotion to playing as hard as they work. The Japanese people I call my friends are masters of cutting loose.

Japanese diners address eating and drinking with purpose and expertise. In my mind, though, enjoying food like a Japanese person doesn't necessarily mean eating more Japanese food. It's about being in touch with the seasons and eating accordingly. In Japan there's a widespread knowledge of what's good to eat and when to get it.

Come October 1, everybody knows they should be eating pike. Then in the spring, everyone's waiting for the first bamboo shoots to start popping up out of the soil. When they go to the market and spot some peanuts grown in Chiba, they know that they're a little more expensive but worth it, because they're really, really delicious.

Of course, recognizing this, Japanese chefs take seasonality to a level that's absolutely bananas, with the hyperluxurious kaiseki restaurants you find in more rural parts of Japan. The food is delicious, but you really go to those places to be among nature—mountains, hot springs, forests, waterfalls. When you're living in a megalopolis like Tokyo, it's important to get out of the city even if only for an afternoon of hiking or fishing, or to see a rural temple, or to admire some birds. Plus, eating in the place where your food comes from is really underrated. A Family-Style Chirashi (page 197) tastes all the better when you eat it at the beach.

Not that I'm doing that every weekend. I'm not going to pretend I'm some kind of woodsy outdoors-man. I love going to restaurants and bars. I'm a sucker for a well-made cocktail, an interesting bottle of wine, and lots of snacks. If you can give me all three simultaneously, all the better.

Which brings me to another feature of the Japanese approach to fun that I love: the seamless relationship between eating and drinking. In America a question that usually gets asked when you're making plans to go out for drinks with friends is, "Do they have food?" And then: Is it a bar or a restaurant? What kind of bar or restaurant is it? Is it a cocktail bar? A wine bar? A dive bar? Do they have booze, or just wine and beer? Should I eat beforehand? Or should we just grab a bite afterward?

It's not as though these distinctions are absent in Japan—in fact, they might be even more pronounced—but there's much less guesswork involved with going out. In Japan I've come to expect that the place I'm visiting will have sorted out the ideal relationship between the drinks and food they serve.

At your average bar, you might nibble on little fried fish or pickles or a hunk of boiled sweet potato in between beers. Those drinking snacks are called *otsumami*, and they serve to keep your palate awake and prevent you from becoming famished while you drink. (I shudder to think of all the dirty bowls of stale Chex Mix or Goldfish crackers or peanuts I've eaten outside of Japan.) At serious soba shops—the kind where the chefs grow and mill their own buckwheat—you don't just go in, eat your noodles, and leave. You sit down and you drink sake. You have a little grilled fish, a little salad, some otsumami. More sake. Finally, at the end of the meal,

Top left: The super-fun and very old-fashioned Kamiya Bar in Asakusa.
Top right: Enjoying a glass of shochu between sushi courses.
Bottom right: An array of opportunities for good times.
Bottom left: Chicken skewers flanked by cold beer.

At Kamiya Bar, it's beer for me, and the house aperitif (called Denki Bran) for Mari.

you have your impeccable soba. At yakitori joints, skewers of grilled chicken are always accompanied by beer or shochu or a cold highball. And with the exception of the intensely ritualistic places, when you go out for sushi, you're really doing some serious drinking in the form of various sakes and shochus, punctuated with the occasional beer or sparkling wine.

The izakaya is the pinnacle of what we've come to define in America as a "gastropub"—places where food and drink flow together smoothly and continuously. When you sit down at an izakaya (or a kappo restaurant, which is somewhere between izakaya and kaiseki), you'll sip on a beer while you snack on small plates of fresh tofu or marinated vegetables or tiny fish mixed with grated daikon. Then you'll proceed to a few slices of the day's best sashimi, accompanied by a glass of sake. As the dishes get a little more

substantial, the sake might get a little drier. Or maybe the chef will take you in a completely different direction and pour some yuzu-infused liqueur. It doesn't feel as precious or ceremonial as a wine pairing— it's more obvious and natural.

Thanks to smart, enterprising chefs in the States, this sort of easy relationship between food and drink is becoming more common in American restaurants, but I'm still surprised by the number of Americans who have a rigid distinction in their minds between drinks and dinner. I don't want to come off as a boozehound, because I'm actually a lightweight. This chapter is simply about being better equipped to entertain people, with a few snacks to serve with drinks, a noodle dish for late nights, and one trick for getting people out of your house when it's time to wrap things up (see Giant Sushi, page 200).

Daikon–Pickled Plum Salad (Daikon Sarada)

Serves 4 as a drinking snack

Along with a plate of pickles, daikon salad is the snack I've come across most often in izakayas. It's a really understated dish, but an amazing thing to munch on with drinks before a meal. Unlike a lot of other "appetizers" (looking at you, fried potato skins), a daikon salad truly piques your appetite. The umeboshi have a tremendous amount of umami and acidity from fermentation, and the daikon is just substantial enough that it's a pleasure to graze on without filling you up.

1 small (8 ounces) daikon

3 medium or 5 small (1 ounce) umeboshi (pickled plums), pitted and minced

2 teaspoons vegetable oil

1 teaspoon rice vinegar

½ teaspoon honey

4 shiso or mint leaves, cut into ribbons

1 tablespoon sesame seeds

1. Peel the daikon and slice it into ⅛-inch-thick matchsticks. (If you have a mandoline that can julienne, use that.) Taste the daikon. If it's especially astringent or spicy, you may want to soak it in a bowl of ice water for an hour to mellow it out.

2. Whisk together the umeboshi, oil, rice vinegar, and honey in a medium bowl. Drain the daikon thoroughly if you soaked it, and add it to the bowl. Toss to combine, then fold in the shiso or mint and sesame seeds. Serve.

Daikon and Cucumber "Sandwiches" with Shiso and Pickled Plums

Serves 8 as a drinking snack

There are basically two kinds of izakayas. There's the classic utilitarian izakaya that serves the same forty or so things you know and love: agedashi tofu, fried chicken (karaage), grilled mackerel (saba), Potato Salad (Potato Sarada, page 178), Grilled Rice Balls (Yaki Onigiri, page 186). Then there are the more ambitious chef-driven izakayas that riff on those classic dishes using seasonal ingredients.

These "sandwiches" are the sort of thing you might find at the latter kind of izakaya. Daikon salad with umeboshi and shiso leaves is a common enough dish (page 177), but here it's rejiggered so that you experience the same blend of sourness and freshness in a different textural context.

A mandoline will make this recipe much easier, but it's not necessary. More important is that you find daikon and cucumbers that are the same thickness throughout (rather than tapering from fat to thin). You'll be slicing rounds of daikon and cucumber to form the "bread" of the sandwiches, and it'll be easier if the top and bottom of the sandwich are the same size.

One 4-inch piece daikon, about
   1½ inches in diameter
1 English cucumber
5 to 6 small umeboshi (pickled
   plums) or 1 ounce umeboshi
   paste
½ teaspoon honey
½ teaspoon rice vinegar
¼ teaspoon shichimi togarashi
20 shiso leaves

1. Peel the daikon and use a mandoline or sharp knife to cut 20 thin rounds, each about ¹⁄₁₆ inch thick. Place the slices in a bowl of ice water to keep them crisp and prevent them from oxidizing.

2. Peel off as much of the cucumber skin as you like—a few strips is enough, but you can go completely nude if you want. Slice the cuke into 20 rounds that are about twice as thick as the daikon.

3. Remove the pits from the whole pickled plums, if using, and chop the flesh into a fine paste. Mix the umeboshi paste with the honey, vinegar, and togarashi in a bowl.

4. Remove the daikon slices from the water and pat dry with paper towels. For each daikon sandwich, spread a thin layer of plum paste on one slice of daikon, top with a whole shiso leaf, and finish with another slice of daikon. Do the same for the cucumber. If your shiso leaves are especially large, trim them to fit the sandwiches. Serve immediately.

Potato Salad (Potato Sarada)

Serves 4 to 6 as a drinking snack

Potato salad is probably as popular in Japan as it is in America. In Japan it's not just a thing you eat at summer picnics; it shows up in bento boxes and on convenience store shelves year-round. Almost without fail, every izakaya has its version of it. At Kotaro, one of my favorite places in Tokyo, the chef serves a scoop of his potato salad with a soft-boiled egg on top, just in case you were worried it wasn't rich enough.

The basic idea of potato salad in Japan isn't very different from what you'd find at the Sam's Club in Iowa: mayonnaise-y, a little sweet, and soft enough for babies and old-timers alike. Obviously, Kewpie mayo gives things an extra punch of umami, and the potato salad in Japan tends to be more mashed than what we're used to in America. This recipe comes from my wife's family. They only mash half the potatoes for more textural variety and toss in some caramelized onions for good measure.

2 medium russet potatoes (1½ pounds), peeled and sliced into 2-inch chunks

1 medium carrot, peeled, halved lengthwise, and cut into ⅛-inch-thick slices

1 tablespoon unsalted butter

1 medium onion, sliced thin

¼ cup Kewpie mayonnaise

1 tablespoon brown sugar

1½ teaspoons kosher salt

1 teaspoon rice vinegar

1. Place the potatoes in a medium saucepan, cover with cold water by 1 inch, and bring to a simmer over medium-high heat. Drop the heat to low and simmer until the potatoes are fork-tender, about 15 minutes. Use a slotted spoon or spider to transfer the potatoes to a colander to cool.

2. Add the carrot to the simmering water and cook until tender, 3 to 4 minutes. Drain, reserving ⅓ cup of the cooking liquid.

3. Heat a large skillet over medium heat, then add the butter. Once the butter stops foaming, add the onion and sauté until softened and lightly browned, about 10 minutes. Remove from the heat and let cool.

4. Add half the potatoes to a bowl and use a fork to smash them into a chunky mash. Add the rest of the potatoes, the reserved cooking liquid, the onion, mayonnaise, brown sugar, salt, and rice vinegar and mix well, then stir in the carrot and check the seasoning. Serve immediately, or store in the fridge for up to a couple days before serving.

Sautéed Chicken Livers with Garlic Chives (Reba Nira)

Serves 4 as a drinking snack

I'm not going to waste time trying to convince you of the merits of liver. If you don't like it, look away. But if you're one of the enlightened among us, this is a great little Chinese-style sauté of chicken livers and oniony garlic chives. It's a pretty classic dish in Japan, where you'll find it in teishoku-ya (diners) and Chinese noodle shops, but in my mind, it's best eaten as beer food. You set out a communal plate, hand out some chopsticks, and chat with your friends while snacking and sipping.

There's a fantastic mix of textures going on here, with the creamy liver and the slight crunch left in the bean sprouts and the garlic chives. The sauce is pure sweet-savory goodness, which takes the edge off the mild bitterness of the liver. Eaten with a bowl of steamed rice, this dish can be a full meal.

12 ounces chicken livers

1 cup milk

1 teaspoon toasted sesame oil

3 tablespoons plus 1 teaspoon sake

2 tablespoons plus 1 teaspoon soy
    sauce

1 tablespoon oyster sauce

2 teaspoons sugar

2 tablespoons potato starch or
    cornstarch

2 tablespoons vegetable oil

2 tablespoons minced garlic

2 tablespoons minced ginger

12 ounces garlic chives (nira),
    sliced into 1-inch lengths

12 ounces bean sprouts, rinsed

1. Clean the chicken livers by separating each one into two lobes and trimming off any tough connective tissue. Place the livers in a bowl and cover with the milk. Let soak for 1 hour.

2. Drain the livers and rinse briefly under cold water. Rinse out the bowl and give it a quick pat dry, then return the livers to the bowl and add the sesame oil, 1 teaspoon of the sake, and 1 teaspoon of the soy sauce. Mix gently and allow to marinate in the fridge for at least 30 minutes or up to 1 hour.

3. Combine the remaining 3 tablespoons sake and 2 tablespoons soy sauce, the oyster sauce, and sugar in a bowl and stir to dissolve the sugar. Set aside.

4. Transfer the marinated livers to a shallow dish or plate and dust with the starch. Heat a large skillet over medium-high heat, then coat with 1 tablespoon of the vegetable oil. Add the livers in a single layer and cook, turning once, until browned and nearly cooked through, about 2 minutes per side. Scoop out of the pan and set aside.

5. Wipe the pan clean with a paper towel and return to medium-high heat. Coat with the remaining 1 tablespoon vegetable oil, add the garlic and ginger, and cook until aromatic, about 1 minute. Add the garlic chives and sauté for 2 minutes, then stir in the bean sprouts and cook until they're just beginning to wilt, about 1 minute more.

6. Return the cooked livers to the pan and add the reserved sauce mixture. Give everything a toss to combine and cook until the sauce bubbles and thickens slightly, about 2 minutes. Serve immediately.

Grilled Peppers
with Ginger-Onion Shio Tare

Serves 4 to 6 as an appetizer

One night when Chris and I were tooling around Kyoto with our families, a friend invited us to dinner at his favorite izakaya, Kiharu. We were blown away, first when we realized that Kiharu-san, the chef, had come in on his day off to cook for us, and then again once we started eating his brilliant, vegetable-focused cooking. This dish of assorted peppers, lightly grilled and smothered in a gingery shio tare, was a standout.

I had never really thought to use shio tare this way before. At Ivan Ramen, our shio tare is a salty sofrito of onion, garlic, and apple that serves as the flavor base of our classic shio ramen. (*Shio* is Japanese for "salt.") This version was inspired by Kiharu. It's much less salty and could be slathered over all sorts of vegetables or even a piece of fish. The recipe makes more tare than you need for the peppers, but it'll keep in the fridge for a week, during which time you'll undoubtedly find other uses for it, or other things to smear it on (roasted potatoes and mushrooms, fried cauliflower, grilled lettuces).

Bear in mind that different kinds of salt have different levels of saltiness. Sea salts tend to be less salty, so if you decide to use kosher salt instead, consider easing back a little bit. As always, let taste be your guide.

SHIO TARE

½ cup plus 1 tablespoon
  vegetable oil

½ onion, finely diced

4 garlic cloves, minced

One 1-inch piece ginger, peeled
  and minced

1 to 2 teaspoons fine sea salt

3 bell peppers (or 12–15 small,
  sweet peppers) of various colors

1. **FOR THE SHIO TARE:** Combine the oil, onion, garlic, and ginger in a small heavy-bottomed saucepan, set over low heat, and cook for about 20 minutes, stirring occasionally, until the onion has softened and barely begun to brown.

2. Remove the pan from the heat and add 5 tablespoons water and 1 teaspoon salt, stirring to dissolve the salt. Cool to room temperature, then taste and decide whether or not to add more salt.

3. Prepare a medium fire in an outdoor grill or preheat the oven to 400°F.

4. If you're using large peppers, stem them, remove the seeds, and slice into quarters. Grill over medium heat or roast on a baking sheet, turning occasionally, until the skins have begun to blacken in places and the flesh is tender but not completely limp, about 20 minutes. Arrange the peppers on a plate and top generously with the shio tare. Serve warm.

Chicken Meatballs (Tsukune)

Serves 6 to 8 as an appetizer

In Japan, tsukune are a yakitori thing. When your restaurant specializes in grilling skewered chicken parts, you're going to have a lot of scraps that can be ground up for meatballs. But tsukune isn't something I've seen made at home very often. For one thing, most people I know in Japan don't grill at home. They'll pack up a little portable grill and take it to the park in the summer, but grillin' and chillin' is not a daily summertime ritual.

I'm pretty lazy about getting the grill fired up too, so this recipe for tsukune is designed to be made in a frying pan. If you can't do without the taste of smoke and flame, feel free to grill them over a medium-hot fire, brushing them with the sauce mixture as they cook. Let the meatballs sit long enough on each side so that the sugar caramelizes and the meat gets a little bit of char, but move them to a cooler part of the grill if they start to flame up. Whichever way you cook them, when they're glistening and cooked through, serve them with a raw egg yolk for dipping—it closes the circle of chicken life and brings a nice hit of richness.

MEATBALLS

14 ounces ground chicken

½ onion, finely chopped

One 1-inch piece ginger, peeled and finely grated

½ cup panko

1½ teaspoons potato starch or cornstarch

1 large egg white

1 teaspoon kosher salt

SAUCE

¼ cup soy sauce

2 tablespoons sake

2 tablespoons mirin

2 teaspoons sugar

2 tablespoons vegetable oil

GARNISHES

Shichimi togarashi

1 raw egg yolk (of a quality and freshness you feel comfortable eating raw) per diner

1. **FOR THE MEATBALLS:** Combine the chicken, onion, ginger, panko, starch, egg white, and salt in a bowl and mix thoroughly. Use your hands to form the mixture into 1-ounce (golf ball–size) balls or torpedoes and set aside.

2. **FOR THE SAUCE:** Combine the soy sauce, sake, mirin, and sugar in a bowl and stir to dissolve the sugar.

3. Heat a large nonstick or well-seasoned carbon steel skillet over medium-high heat, then coat with the vegetable oil. Place the meatballs in the pan and cook for 7 to 8 minutes, turning them often so they brown evenly on all sides.

4. When the meatballs are just about perfectly done, turn the heat up and pour the sauce mixture into the pan. Swirl the pan back and forth to coat the tsukune in the sauce, then cook for 3 more minutes, allowing the liquid to reduce and glaze the meat. Serve hot, with a sprinkling of togarashi and raw egg yolks for dipping.

Savory Pancakes (Okonomiyaki)

Serves 4 as a drinking snack

If you're familiar with okonomiyaki, chances are you know it as a clean-out-the-fridge franken-pancake stuffed with cabbage and a multitude of other ingredients, such as onion, scallions, pork belly or bacon, seafood, fish cakes, udon, mochi (rice cakes), and/or basically anything else you can think of. (As you might guess, it's usually something you scarf down during a night of drinking.) Okonomiyaki are well loved all over Japan, but Hiroshima and Osaka are especially famous for their regional versions. There, these pancakes can grow to several inches in thickness and normally come garnished with copious squiggles of Kewpie mayo and Bull-Dog sauce, as well as katsuobushi (bonito flakes) that wave and wilt in the steam, as though they have a life of their own.

We lived in Tokyo, where the okonomiyaki tend to be a more spartan affair. This version is made only with cabbage and thin slices of pork belly, but feel free to gussy it up with whatever you like (or make it vegetarian by omitting the pork belly and katsuobushi). It's mercifully simple and can be prepared with minimal fuss, even after partaking of a couple adult beverages.

1 cup all-purpose flour

2½ teaspoons baking powder

1½ teaspoons sugar

1 teaspoon kosher salt

1 large egg

1 tablespoon vegetable oil (plus an additional 2 tablespoons if making a vegetarian version)

2¼ cups tightly packed shredded green cabbage

11 ounces thinly sliced skinless pork belly (see Thinly Sliced Meat, page 129) or uncured bacon

GARNISHES

Kewpie mayonnaise

Bull-Dog tonkatsu sauce

Aonori (powdered dried green seaweed)

Chopped scallions

Katsuobushi (bonito flakes)

1. Combine the flour, baking powder, sugar, and salt in a medium bowl. Whisk the egg and 1 tablespoon oil together with ¾ cup water in another bowl. Add the wet ingredients to the dry and mix briefly until most of the lumps of dry flour are gone. Fold in the shredded cabbage.

2. Set a nonstick skillet over medium-high heat and lay 3 strips of pork belly or bacon next to each other in it. Once the pork begins to sizzle, let it cook for 2 minutes to render some of the fat. Spoon half the batter on top and spread into a ½-inch-thick layer. (If you're making a vegetarian version, coat the pan with a tablespoon of vegetable oil before adding the batter.)

3. Cook for 3 to 4 minutes, then sneak a peek underneath. Once the bottom is crisp and brown, give the pancake a flip with a spatula. Do it confidently and quickly to avoid making a mess. Cook for another 3 to 4 minutes, until the okonomiyaki is golden brown on both sides. The inside should be cooked through, but it's fine if it's still a bit moist—the cabbage will give up a fair amount of water.

4. Slide the okonomiyaki onto a plate and top freely with squiggles of Kewpie mayo and Bull-Dog sauce. Sprinkle with aonori, scallions, and a big handful of katsuobushi (unless you've made a vegetarian version). Serve immediately, then use the remaining pork and batter to make and serve the second okonomiyaki.

Grilled Rice Balls (Yaki Onigiri)

Serves 4 as a drinking snack

I always forget that I've ordered yaki onigiri. I'll be at an izakaya, finishing up my last beer, when, invariably, out comes a plate of beautifully bronzed rice balls. Most people might find delight in such a surprise. Because I'm kind of a curmudgeon, I find it slightly annoying when something takes so long to cook that I forgot I ordered it.

That's the thing about yaki onigiri, though. They are a labor of love. To make them correctly—crisp on the outside, warm and steamy on the inside—there's no substitute for standing over the stove, flipping and basting them over low heat. Don't get me wrong, it's totally worth it. I struggle to think of a better bite to accompany cold beer than a yaki onigiri dragged through mentaiko mayo. Especially when you haven't forgotten it's coming.

If you like, you can cook yaki onigiri over a wire rack set over a low burner or on a grill—just be sure the heat is extremely low.

2 to 3 tablespoons vegetable oil

4 Rice Balls (Onigiri, page 56), freshly made

2 tablespoons Dashi (page 28)

2 teaspoons soy sauce

1 teaspoon mirin

FOR SERVING

Mentaiko Mayo (optional; recipe follows)

1. Heat a nonstick skillet over medium-low heat, then coat with a little of the vegetable oil. Gently lay the onigiri in the pan and allow to cook while you mix together the dashi, soy sauce, and mirin in a small bowl.

2. Brush the onigiri lightly with the dashi-soy mixture, then flip them over. Keep brushing and flipping every few minutes until top and bottom are crisp and brown, about 20 minutes, adding more oil as needed. Serve hot with lots of mentaiko mayo, if you've made it.

Mentaiko Mayo

Makes about ⅓ cup

2 ounces mentaiko (cod or pollock roe), gently scraped from the sac

¼ cup Kewpie mayonnaise

Mix the mentaiko and mayonnaise thoroughly together in a bowl. Serve immediately.

Spicy Somen with Poached Chicken

Serves 4

While we were shooting the photos for this book, I had to take a day off from our set in Chris's in-laws' house in Sonoma County to give a TED Talk. I've told the story of my ramen journey plenty of times, but something about doing it in the TED setting made me nervous, so when I got back, I felt a huge sense of relief. To celebrate, Chris threw together this badass dish from ingredients that were lying around. We had a bunch of somen on hand because we'd made grand plans to build a somen slide,* but we ended up running out of time. We'd also whipped up a big batch of Chunky Chili Oil (Taberu Rayu, page 234) and were basically slathering it on everything we could. Spicy somen was a logical next step: cold noodles, poached chicken, and loads of chunky, spicy oil. This has since become a staple of late-night meals and afternoon picnics in both of our homes.

*Wait, wait, wait, wait. What's a somen slide? Glad you asked. I learned about this from my sons after they came home from summer camp in Japan one day and told us about how they'd built a nagashi-somen slide: a long, sloped bamboo trough into which the counselors poured water and chilled somen. The kids lined up along the slide and used chopsticks to pluck out the noodles as they streamed by, dipped them in broth (Tsuketsuyu, page 35), and slurped them up. The slides don't have to be made from bamboo—we'd planned to make ours from a rain gutter—in case you're thinking of tackling one as a weekend project.

---

1 boneless, skinless chicken breast (about 1 pound)

2 tablespoons kosher salt

7 ounces dried somen noodles

1 tablespoon plus 1 teaspoon soy sauce

1 tablespoon rice vinegar

1 teaspoon sugar

1 cup Chunky Chili Oil (Taberu Rayu, page 234)

3 scallions, sliced thin

One 2-inch piece English cucumber, peeled and sliced into matchsticks

1. Combine the chicken breast, 1 tablespoon of the salt, and 6 cups water in a large saucepan set over medium heat and bring to a bare simmer. Immediately drop the heat as low as it will go and cook until the chicken is cooked through, about 25 minutes. Remove the chicken and allow to rest on a plate. (If you like, you can do this a day in advance; wrap the chicken in plastic and chill it in the fridge overnight.)

2. Pour out the poaching liquid (you can strain it and keep for sipping or cooking purposes, if you like), clean out the saucepan, and fill with fresh water. Bring to a boil and season with the remaining 1 tablespoon salt, then add the somen and cook according to the package directions. Meanwhile, set up an ice bath; make sure to use plenty of ice and water, as you want your noodles to chill thoroughly. Once they're cooked, drain the noodles and plunge into the ice bath. Give them a stir with your fingers or a pair of chopsticks and allow to cool for a couple minutes.

3. Once the noodles are ice-cold, drain them really well and place them in a bowl. Add the soy sauce, vinegar, and sugar and mix well.

4. Divide the dressed somen among four plates and top each with a few generous spoonfuls of chili oil. Cut the chicken into ½-inch-thick slices and shingle on top of the noodles. Finish each with a sprinkling of scallions and a handful of cucumber. Serve.

Instant Ramen Party

Serves as many as you like

It took a lot of trials and a healthy amount of error for me to cook a bowl of ramen I was proud to serve at my restaurants. Nowadays at Ivan Ramen, the simplest bowl of shio ramen contains no fewer than ten different components—noodles made with rye flour, chicken schmaltz, seasoning sauces, two kinds of broth, and various toppings—all made from scratch with very specific ingredients. If you want to re-create this meticulous brand of *kodawari ramen* (which translates loosely as "specially crafted artisanal ramen"), Chris and I wrote a whole book about how to do it. You should buy it!

But that's not what this recipe is about. This recipe is for people who can't dedicate a whole weekend to making their own noodles, or who live in a place where fresh ramen noodles are hard to come by. Rather than making a big project out of ramen, we're gussying up instant noodles to approximate the real deal.

In Japan there are countless brands of instant ramen. (In fact, when I was running my shops in Tokyo, I had my own brand of instant ramen that sold out every year.) In Japan, instant ramen occupies basically the same function as it does here: a quick, dirt-cheap meal. At any convenience store, you can pick up a couple packages of noodles and a few fresh ingredients from the refrigerated section to make yourself an eminently slurpable bowl of noodles.

It's in that spirit that we present the Instant Ramen Party. The idea is to serve your guests instant ramen in fresh soup, with whatever toppings and seasonings you feel like throwing together. It's the sort of thing you can set up ahead of time and share with friends after a night out, or a nice way to feed your family a bunch of leftovers. Kids like it because they get to customize their own bowls. It's fun for a dinner party too, especially if you ask everyone to bring their favorite brand of instant ramen to the party.

But the true beauty of this approach is that your guests can be as reckless and over-the-top as they want. This isn't a delicate bowl of ramen. You want your ramen super-spicy? Add a fat scoop of Chunky Chili Oil (Taberu Rayu, page 234). Prefer your noodles dry? Use less broth and lots of toppings. Like eggs? Add two. Or three. Nobody's judging you.

SOUP
For each bowl:

1 cup Dashi (your choice, page 28)
1 cup chicken stock, homemade or store-bought

SEASONINGS
You can offer all of these to your guests, but instruct them to choose only two or three. As a guideline, the measurements that follow are for 2 cups of soup.

The seasoning packets that come with the ramen
2 teaspoons miso of your choice
1 teaspoon katsuobushi (bonito flakes), ground to a fine powder in a spice grinder
½ teaspoon fine sea salt
1 teaspoon soy sauce

1 teaspoon brine from Pickled Garlic (page 232)
2 teaspoons Ginger-Onion Shio Tare (page 181)
½ teaspoon rendered pork or chicken fat
½ teaspoon toasted sesame oil
½ teaspoon Japanese chili oil (rayu) or Chunky Chili Oil (Taberu Rayu, page 234)
1 teaspoon unsalted butter

NOODLES

You're looking for packs of instant ramen where the noodles and seasonings are kept separate, not the Styrofoam cups of premixed noodles with freeze-dried vegetable bits and seasoning.

Salt

1 or 2 packages of instant ramen
    noodles per diner

TOPPINGS

Choose as many as you like. This is a great place to use up leftovers. You can serve things straight out of the fridge—the broth should be hot enough to warm everything through. Or you can heat everything in the microwave or on the stovetop before serving.

Slow-Roasted Tomatoes
    (page 193)
Seasoned Ground Pork
    (page 193)
Simmered Bamboo Tips
    (page 193)
Kimchi Pork Belly (Buta Kimchi,
    page 74)
Panfried Pork Cutlets in Ginger
    Sauce (Shogayaki, page 39)

Chicken Meatballs (Tsukune,
    page 182)
Seasoned Spinach (Ohitashi,
    page 204)

GARNISHES

Hot-Spring Eggs (Onsen Tamago,
    page 30)
Soy-Marinated Eggs (Ajitama,
    page 30)
Pickled Garlic (page 232)
Negi (Japanese green onions)
    or scallions, sliced thin
Nori sheets, quartered

RECIPE CONTINUES

1. Bring 12 cups water to a boil in a large pot and season liberally with salt. Have a strainer standing by for cooking and draining the noodles.

2. Measure out the dashi and chicken broth—1 cup of each per serving. Combine both liquids in a large saucepan and bring to a simmer over medium-high heat, then drop the heat to very low and keep covered.

3. Instruct your diners to start by adding their choice of seasonings to their empty soup bowls. They should feel free to mix and match as they like, but be wary of salt levels: The seasoning packets that come with instant ramen already contain salt, sugar, MSG, and other seasonings. If you love these, use them, but don't use any extra salt or soy sauce. And don't forget to add a little richness in the form of animal fat, oil, or butter.

4. Working with one serving at a time, drop the noodles into the boiling water and cook until al dente—usually 2 to 3 minutes, tops. Meanwhile, ladle 2 cups of soup into each guest's bowl and tell them to stir in the seasonings. Drain the noodles thoroughly and add them to the soup. Let your guests top and garnish the ramen however they like.

Slow-Roasted Tomatoes

Serves 4 as part of a ramen party

I love adding tomatoes to ramen because they have a ton of umami as well as bright acidity. However, when I was living in Japan, the tomatoes were never great (unless I shelled out for the really high-end stuff), so I learned to make the best of mediocre ones by slowly roasting them to concentrate their flavor. If you're in a rush, you can do this at a higher temperature in less time, but the result won't have the same depth of flavor.

2 Roma (plum) tomatoes, halved lengthwise
1 tablespoon plus 1 teaspoon olive oil
1 teaspoon salt
1 garlic clove, minced

1. Preheat the oven to 225°F. Line a baking sheet with parchment.

2. Place the tomatoes in a bowl and drizzle with the olive oil. Sprinkle on the salt and garlic and gently toss to combine. Place the tomatoes flesh side down on the baking sheet and slide into the oven. Bake for 3 hours, or until the tomatoes have transformed into wrinkled, softened, flavor-packed versions of themselves.

3. Serve, or cool and store in an airtight container in the fridge for a couple days.

Seasoned Ground Pork

Serves 4 as part of a ramen party

At my restaurants, we serve our ramen with slow-cooked pork belly, but the point of an instant ramen party is to keep things simple. (Not that cooking pork belly is complicated, but it can be daunting if you've never attempted it.) So here's a straightforward pork topping for your instant ramen, seasoned with teriyaki flavors.

1 tablespoon vegetable oil
8 ounces ground pork
1 tablespoon sake
1 tablespoon mirin
1 tablespoon plus 1 teaspoon soy sauce
½ teaspoon sugar

Heat a medium skillet over high heat, then coat with the vegetable oil. Once the oil is hot, add the ground pork and use a spoon or spatula to break up the meat. Let the meat brown for a minute while you stir together the sake, mirin, soy sauce, and sugar in a bowl. Add the seasoning mixture to the pan and cook, constantly stirring and breaking up any clumps of meat, for 3 to 5 minutes, or until the pork is cooked through and the liquid has been mostly absorbed or evaporated. Serve, or cool and store in an airtight container in the fridge for a couple days.

Simmered Bamboo Tips

Serves 10 as part of a ramen party

Your average bowl of Tokyo-style ramen will contain a couple long strands of pickled bamboo, called *menma*. Menma isn't so easy to come by in the States, but you can find cans of boiled bamboo shoot tips in most Asian markets. (I actually prefer their crunchy texture to menma.) After a quick simmer in soy sauce, they're ready to adorn your noodles.

One 19-ounce can whole bamboo shoot tips, drained
¼ cup sake
¼ cup mirin
¼ cup soy sauce
1 tablespoon sugar
½ cup tightly packed katsuobushi (bonito flakes)

1. Stand each bamboo tip on its flat end and slice it lengthwise in half. Lay each half on the cut side and slice into ¼-inch-wide strips. Rinse under cold water.

2. Combine the bamboo, sake, mirin, soy sauce, sugar, and 1 cup water in a small saucepan and bring to a simmer over medium heat. Cook for 10 minutes, then shut off the heat and add the katsuobushi. Allow to cool to room temperature, then drain the shoots, scraping off any katsuobushi that clings to them. Serve, or store in an airtight container in the fridge for up to a week.

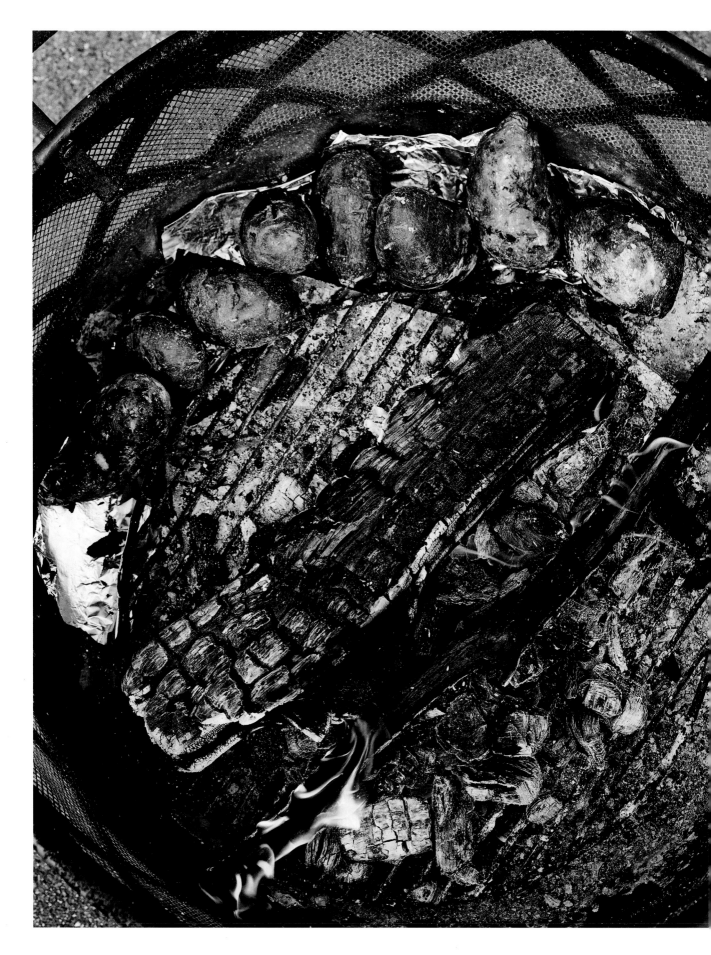

Fire-Roasted Sweet Potatoes (Yaki Imo)

Serves as many as you like

When my wife and I first started living together in Japan, she had a great job as a freelance interior designer. She'd travel around filming lifestyle shoots, redecorating famous actors' houses, or showing people how they could organize their cars more efficiently (yes, it's a thing). Meanwhile, I was more or less just loafing around, taking care of the kids and tagging along where I could.

Mari did a lot of work with magazine editors—those hip, intellectual types who'd done a requisite stint in New York or Paris or Rome or wherever. One fall day, the editor of one of the fashion and lifestyle magazine invited us to a party at his parents' house—a three-acre spread a little outside the famous port city of Yokohama. (Once you get outside of Tokyo proper, there's actually quite a bit of open space.) The place was surrounded by woods, and they had a small farm with chickens roaming around and a nice plot of herbs and vegetables.

The party was outdoors in the sunshine—a big family gathering with everyone's wives and husbands and kids. The adults were all drinking beer, and the kids were playing games, and everyone was chipping in with the cooking. At one point, the adults told the kids to start digging up sweet potatoes, and they happily set to pulling potatoes out of the soil with little garden tools. They washed the potatoes off at the spigot and handed them to their parents, who wrapped them in foil and stuck them straight into the fire. The potatoes cooked lazily all afternoon as the party went on. There was an enormous outdoor rice cooker, with a weathered wooden lid and two-by-fours for handles, in which someone made a huge batch of Takikomi Gohan (page 116). Another guest grilled whole fish with the guts still intact, so they came out a little bitter and salty and delicious. Someone else oversaw a big cauldron of Tonjiru (Pork and Miso-Ginger Stew; page 119) that we ladled into bowls and cracked fresh eggs into. And just as everything was coming together for dinner, the potatoes were ready.

Plucked out of the coals and unswaddled from their foil, the potatoes sent out billows of steam as we cracked them open. The afternoon had given way to a slightly chilly evening, and having those potatoes in our hands warmed us through. The flesh was pale yellow, creamy, perfectly sweet, nutty, and a little smoky from the flames. Until that moment, my experience with sweet potatoes had been restricted to Thanksgiving casseroles topped with marshmallows. I don't want to be disrespectful to my Southern brethren, but once you've had a properly roasted Japanese sweet potato, you'll never settle for brown sugar–sweetened orange mush again.

Those unadorned sweet potatoes, as simple as could be, were a revelation to me. Not just their remarkable deliciousness, but the way in which the whole process of digging them up and cooking them had come so naturally to everyone at the party. They were all plugged in to what was good to eat at that time of year and how to cook it. It was fall, so of course we'd have sweet potatoes. There was a splendid knowingness. It was a big deal to me, at least.

I admit, this idyllic countryside party was a little fantastical, but it made a strong impression on me. I imagine it's the same sort of revelatory farm-to-table dining experience that Alice Waters was having in the sixties in France and Italy. Where Waters saw a philosophy she could bring back to America, I took something slightly more selfish from my sweet-potato encounter.

Japanese city dwellers are just as hyperattuned to seasonality as people in the countryside. In the middle of November, trucks start popping up all over Tokyo with vendors shouting, *"Yaki imo!*"—"Baked sweet potato!"—and selling hot roasted tubers for a few bucks apiece. And down the block from where we lived, there was a really cool market and a great fishmonger. I was jobless and just kind of floating around Japan. I spoke the language well enough, but I didn't really feel like I could call myself Japanese. I was shy and not fully acclimated to Tokyo life. But I started feeling more and more comfortable walking into these markets and talking to the shopkeepers about what was new and ripe and ideal to eat. It made me feel Japanese in a way that transcended my shaky language skills or skin color or general awkwardness. In a very real way, eating a roasted sweet potato out on the farm was my first step toward starting my own business in Japan.

In America we're at more of a disadvantage when it comes to connecting with nature through our food. If you do most of your grocery shopping at huge supermarket chains, you'd be forgiven for thinking that strawberries and tomatoes were in season year-round. I'm not advocating that everybody upend their lives to become locavores. In fact, I think it's become something of an elitist—not to mention expensive and difficult—thing to do in America. Not all of us live near the San Francisco Ferry Building or want to schlep a backpack full of twenty pounds of vegetables. I get it. But it's easy to get disconnected from where your food comes from and when it's really fresh and ripe and in season.

Here's what I think you can do. Choose one local seasonal ingredient and look forward to it every year. It can be anything—cold-water shellfish in the winter, chestnuts, a variety of apple, persimmons, morel mushrooms. Make a point of knowing when that ingredient shows up in stores, getting some, and enjoying it. Or, if you have access to a little land, try growing something that does well in your area. You'll learn what it means for a plant to grow and change through the year, when it's too early to harvest, and when it's perfect. It takes a bit of effort, but once you've done it, you'll feel so much more connected not only to your food, but also to where you live.

These days my family and I reside in the lower Hudson Valley, which produces some of the best food in the country. There are great little breweries and cideries and cheesemakers all over the place, and every fall we get some of the country's most beautiful apples. There's a local cider that comes around every October and that's what my family and I drink all season long. It reminds me of my childhood on Long Island, drinking cider from apples pressed at the local mill. It's my little chosen gesture that keeps me feeling like a native New Yorker. It's funny how a roasted sweet potato in Japan taught me to ground myself as an American.

Japanese sweet potatoes, one per person

Wash and gently scrub the potatoes. Build a fire in the center of a firepit or barbecue and let it burn for a while. You're looking for some white coals to accumulate. Use a long pair of tongs (or a heat-proof glove) to place the potatoes around the fire, 6 to 8 inches from the coals. Let the potatoes cook for about 1 hour, feeding the fire as necessary to keep things burning. Watch the potatoes carefully and turn them often. If they look like they're charring before they've cooked through, wrap them loosely in foil and return them to the fire. As they cook, the potatoes may crack and release sugary juices that will caramelize on the skin—don't worry about it. They're done when they're soft to the touch and the skins feel crunchy. Let them cool slightly before wrapping them individually in napkins or newspaper and handing them out. Crack them open, inhale the steam, and enjoy.

Family-Style Chirashi

Serves 4

In the States, when you order chirashi, ninety-nine times out of a hundred, you're going to get a bowl of rice topped with an assortment of sashimi and fish roe meant to feed one person. This family-style version is something I see much more often in Japan, where families will gather around a big platter of vinegared rice covered with various types of seafood and vegetables for a shared picnic lunch. Along with a Temaki Party (page 64), chirashi is one of my family's favorite ways to eat sushi without breaking our backs shaping and rolling rice.

You can top chirashi with whatever ingredients you like. This one is heavy on the vegetables, but if you want to add more sliced fish, feel free. For special occasions like New Year's, we'll make a decadent one covered entirely with ikura (cured salmon roe) and nothing else.

4 cups Sushi Rice (page 26)

Sweet Egg Ribbons (Kinshi Tamago, page 199)

Soy-Marinated Tuna (Maguro Zuke, page 32), sliced into strips

Sake-Steamed Shrimp (Ebi no Sakamushi, at right)

Seasoned Shiitake Mushrooms (Shiitake no Amakara ni, page 199), cut into ¼-inch-thick slices

½ English cucumber, quartered lengthwise and sliced thin

5 ounces ikura (cured salmon roe)

Lotus Root Pickles (Renkon no Tsukemono, page 199)

FOR SERVING

Soy sauce

Wasabi paste (from a tube is fine)

Pickled sushi ginger

Spread the rice in an even layer in a casserole dish or large bowl. Scatter the egg ribbons over the rice, then arrange the rest of the ingredients on top. Serve family-style with soy sauce, wasabi, and sushi ginger on the side.

Sake-Steamed Shrimp (Ebi no Sakamushi)

Makes ½ pound

¼ cup plus 1 tablespoon sake

¼ teaspoon kosher salt

8 ounces medium shrimp in the shell

Combine the sake and salt in a small saucepan and set over high heat. As soon as the sake begins to simmer, add the shrimp, stir, and cover the pan. Wait 1 minute, then shut off the heat and allow to stand for 6 to 8 minutes, depending on the size of your shrimp. Once the shrimp are cooked through, chill them in an ice bath, drain, and peel.

RECIPE CONTINUES

Soy-Marinated Tuna (page 32)

Sake-Steamed Shrimp

Ikura

Sweet Egg Ribbons

Seasoned Shiitake Mushrooms

Lotus Root Pickles

Sweet Egg Ribbons (Kinshi Tamago)

Makes 1 cup

4 large eggs
1 tablespoon sugar
Vegetable oil

1. Whisk the eggs and sugar together in a bowl.

2. Heat a medium nonstick skillet over medium heat, then coat with vegetable oil. Pour in a thin layer of the egg mixture—just enough to cover the bottom of the pan. Let cook for about 1 minute, or until the eggs are set. Flip the omelet onto a cutting board and repeat until you've used up all the egg mixture. Once the cooked omelets are cool, roll them into cylinders and slice them into thin ribbons.

Seasoned Shiitake Mushrooms (Shiitake no Amakara ni)

Makes about ½ cup

10 dried shiitake mushrooms, stems removed
¼ cup sake
¼ cup mirin
¼ cup soy sauce
1 tablespoon sugar

Place the shiitakes in a saucepan and cover with 2 cups cold water. Add the sake, mirin, soy sauce, and sugar, bring to a simmer over medium heat, and cook for 30 minutes, or until the pan is almost completely dry. Remove the shiitakes from the pan, cool, and store in an airtight container in the fridge for up to 1 week.

Lotus Root Pickles (Renkon no Tsukemono)

Makes 12 ounces

12 ounces lotus root, peeled and sliced thin
¾ cup rice vinegar
2 tablespoons sugar
One 1-inch piece ginger, sliced thin
1 teaspoon kosher salt

1. Place the lotus root in a heat-proof bowl or container.

2. Combine the vinegar, sugar, ginger, salt, and 2 cups water in a saucepan and bring to a boil over high heat, stirring to dissolve the sugar, then pour over the lotus root. Allow to cool to room temperature, then drain and serve. Alternatively, store the pickles in the vinegar in a sealed container in the fridge for up to 3 days; drain before serving.

Giant Sushi (Futomaki)

Makes 10 rolls

A futomaki is a big, fat sushi roll. Before your mind wanders to visions of cream cheese, soft-shell crab, spicy tuna, mango, and bacon, let me clarify the difference between futomaki and your average American sushi joint's roll of the day. Generally speaking, futomaki are heavy on vegetables and almost always include a sweet omelet (tamagoyaki). Unlike a Crispy-Crunchy ZZ-Top Roll, a thoughtfully composed, well-made futomaki is a thing of beauty. When you slice into it, you'll see a variety of colorful ingredients bundled tightly next to one another, like a pane of stained glass.

Futomaki are terrific in bento boxes for kids and as drinking snacks for adults. A while back, after a memorable meal at Yoshitake, the three-Michelin-starred sushi bar in Tokyo, the chef gave each of us a packaged futomaki as a take-home treat. Ever since then, I've also thought of futomaki as a nice way to end the night and shoo away lingering dinner guests.

What follows are some loose-but-detailed guidelines for making futomaki. Once you make your own, you'll get a clearer idea of what ingredients you like. The tamagoyaki is de rigueur, but the rest is up to you—four or five fillings should be enough, but feel free to go as crazy as you like. (I'll emphasize that the sakura ebi—little dried shrimp—are worth seeking out.) I'd only advise you to stay away from wet fillings, as they will bleed through the nori and make a mess. Otherwise, anything is fair game. (My wife insists that fish and meat have no place in futomaki, but I can't help myself.)

The bulk of the time required to make futomaki comes down to prepping ingredients. Get everything cooked, sliced, and organized before you even think about busting out the sushi mat.

In general the goal is to get the fillings to a place where they can easily be laid in a long row down the center of the roll. Try to slice ingredients like cucumber, carrot, pickled daikon, and the tamagoyaki into pieces that are as close in length as possible to the sheet of nori. Don't stress too much, though. You can always lay shorter pieces end to end and trim as necessary.

YOU'LL NEED

10 or 20 sheets sushi nori, depending on your rolling style

6 cups Sushi Rice (page 26), at room temperature

¼ cup roasted sesame seeds

½ ounce sakura ebi (dried red shrimp; optional but strongly recommended)

1 Seasoned Omelet (Tamagoyaki, page 202), sliced into ½-inch-thick batons

PLUS 2 OR 3 VEGETABLES...

1 English cucumber, peeled and sliced into ¼-inch-thick batons

1 large carrot, peeled and sliced into ¼-inch-thick batons, blanched for 90 seconds in salted boiling water, drained, and dunked in ice water to cool

10 Seasoned Shiitake Mushrooms (Shiitake no Amakara ni, page 199), cut into ¼-inch-thick slices

1 cup Seasoned Spinach (Ohitashi, page 204), squeezed dry

4 ounces takuan (pickled daikon), sliced into ¼-inch-thick batons

...AND MEAT OR FISH, IF YOU LIKE

6 ounces Teriyaki Beef (page 204)

12 ounces sushi-grade fish (tuna, snapper, flounder, yellowtail, salmon, or cured mackerel are all nice), sliced into long ¼- to ½-inch-thick strips

EQUIPMENT

Bamboo sushi mat

RECIPE CONTINUES

1. **FOR EACH ROLL:** Lay a long piece of plastic wrap on a clean sushi mat and place a sheet of nori, shiny side down, on top—if your nori has perforated lines in it, position the sheet so that the lines run perpendicular to your body. Scoop about ¾ cup sushi rice onto the nori. Wet your hands with water and gently spread the rice into an even layer, leaving about an inch uncovered at the top.

2. There are two ways you can proceed from here: You can layer the fillings directly onto the rice and roll up the nori or, for a slightly more elegant approach, flip the rice-topped sheet over, layer the fillings onto the nori, roll it up with the rice on the outside, and then wrap in a second piece of nori. Either way, to fill the roll after you've added the rice, sprinkle a spoonful of sesame seeds in a straight line across the center. Follow with a big pinch of sakura ebi, if you have it. Lay a few thick slices of tamagoyaki along the same line, then follow with whatever vegetables and meat you like. Again, the idea is to make a thick roll, so be generous.

3. Lift up the bottom edge of the plastic wrap and bamboo mat to help you roll the sushi from the bottom up, using your fingers to keep the fillings in place if necessary. Seal the uncovered top edge of the nori against the roll. With the plastic wrap covering the roll, drape the bamboo mat over it, and squeeze with firm, even pressure to form the futomaki into a tight cylinder, then roll it back and forth lightly to give it a rounder shape. If you're making a roll with the rice on the outside, remove the plastic and wrap the roll in another piece of nori, then give it the bamboo-mat treatment once more.

4. Use a very sharp knife to cut the roll into 1-inch pieces. If any rice or fillings stick to the knife, wipe it with a wet cloth in between slices to ensure that each piece comes out looking pristine and not like it's been cut with a chainsaw. Repeat with the remaining nori, rice, and fillings. Serve.

Seasoned Omelet (Tamagoyaki)
Makes 1 large omelet

6 large eggs
½ cup Dashi (page 28)
2 teaspoons sugar
2 teaspoons mirin
1 teaspoon soy sauce
½ teaspoon kosher salt
Vegetable oil

EQUIPMENT
Bamboo sushi mat

1. Whisk together the eggs, dashi, sugar, mirin, soy, and salt in a bowl.

2. Heat a 10-inch nonstick skillet over medium-low heat, then coat with a thin layer of vegetable oil. To ensure that the whole pan is evenly coated, you may want to saturate a folded paper towel with oil and use it to spread the oil around. If you're afraid of burning your fingers, use a pair of chopsticks to hold the towel.

3. Pour in ⅓ cup of the egg mixture and let it spread out over the pan. Now don't disturb it until most of the raw egg is cooked. Using a rubber spatula or chopsticks, peel one side of the omelet from the pan and roll it up into a cylinder. (This will take practice, and you may ultimately find that it's easier to use your fingers than a spatula or chopsticks, but we won't advise it lest we open ourselves up to a lawsuit.) If you notice that the bottom of the omelet has browned, your heat is too high. Ideally the eggs will cook through without taking on any color.

4. With the rolled-up omelet resting against one side of the pan, coat the pan with oil again, then pour in another ⅓ cup egg mixture. Lift up the omelet so that some egg can run beneath it, then allow to cook until the new layer of egg is mostly cooked through. Now roll the omelet up in the new layer of egg, like you're a mob enforcer wrapping a snitch in a rug.

5. Repeat step 4 until you've used up the egg mixture.

6. Slide the omelet onto a cutting board. Drape a piece of plastic wrap over it and, while it's still warm, use the bamboo mat to squeeze the omelet into a tight log. Once you're happy with the shape, unwrap the tamagoyaki and allow it to cool before slicing lengthwise into long strips for futomaki.

RECIPE CONTINUES

Seasoned Spinach (Ohitashi)

Makes about 1 cup

Kosher salt

1 pound spinach (or other tender, leafy green)

½ cup Dashi (page 28)

2 tablespoons soy sauce

2 teaspoons mirin

1. Bring a pot of salted water to a boil. Set up an ice bath in a large bowl.

2. Blanch the spinach in the boiling water for 1 to 2 minutes—a shorter bath for baby spinach, longer for hardier leaves—then drain the leaves in a colander and plunge them into the ice bath. Once the spinach is completely cool, drain it, squeeze it with your hands to remove as much water as possible, and transfer to a bowl. Stir in the dashi, soy sauce, and mirin and marinate in the fridge for an hour before serving. Before using the spinach to fill futomaki, give it another good squeeze with your hands to wring out the marinade.

Teriyaki Beef

Makes about 5 ounces

¼ cup soy sauce

¼ cup mirin

2 tablespoons sake

1 tablespoon sugar

1 tablespoon vegetable oil

About 5 ounces thinly sliced rib-eye or chuck roll (see Thinly Sliced Meat, page 129)

1. Combine the soy sauce, mirin, sake, and sugar in a saucepan, bring to a simmer over medium heat, and cook for 2 minutes. Remove from the heat and set aside.

2. Heat a large skillet over high heat, then coat with the vegetable oil. Add the beef and sauté for 2 to 3 minutes, or until it begins to brown and is mostly cooked through. Add the sauce and bring to a simmer, then lower the heat to medium and cook until the sauce has reduced to a syrupy glaze, about 5 minutes. Transfer to a bowl to cool.

3. Once the beef is at room temperature, chop it into small pieces before using as a filling for futomaki.

New Year's

No More Terrible New Year's Parties

I was dubious about New Year's as a holiday for a long time. In America we always talk about turning over a new leaf, but by the third or fourth day of the new year, we've all blown our resolutions. I also never understood why the end of the year meant you should ironically wear a top hat, or party until you black out, or generally act like it's the end of the world.

But when I moved to Japan, something clicked for me about New Year's in a way that had never happened in the States. The first location of Ivan Ramen was in a sleepy suburb called Rokkakoen, on a little street populated by small-business owners—the butcher, the fishmonger, the family who made fresh tofu, my produce lady. Most of them had been doing their jobs for decades. At the end of the year, I could feel their sighs of relief. It's no different from the States, where everybody finally cuts themselves some slack when December rolls around. But in Japan, there was a near-universal happiness, and it made me into a believer. It was celebratory and joyful, but not reckless or self-destructive.

New Year's really begins in November, when you start getting invited to *bonenkai*, year-end parties where you get together with family and colleagues, finalize deals, catch up, and drink. Truth be told, the sheer volume of bonenkai can be a real pain in the ass, but you go to as many as you can, because it's important to show your appreciation for your friends. Also in November, Japanese department stores start rolling out their gift centers with ornate packages of trinkets, good meat and fish, and perfect fruit. And while we all know that the $150 melon probably doesn't taste nineteen times better than the $8 melon, the recipient knows it cost $150 and that's what counts. Gift-giving is essential at New Year's. You deliver presents on December 31 as a gesture of gratitude.

Families use the week leading up to the thirty-first to clean up the whole house. We organize, sweep, scrub, and throw away old crap. On New Year's Eve, we spend the whole day cooking traditional dishes called *osechi ryori*—black beans in syrup, prawns poached in sweet dashi, Japanese sweet potato and chestnuts, whole fish, chicken stuffed with burdock root and carrot. Around midnight, we eat soba, because noodles symbolize longevity. The next day, friends come over and we start the festivities early. I'm not the world's biggest drinker, but by 9 a.m. on New Year's Day, I'm already a couple glasses of sake deep. We bring out different dishes all day, and everybody grazes as they please.

We spend the afternoon talking and laughing and reflecting on the past year, what went right, and what we could've done better. In Japan, the New Year is a time of spiritual reflection, like Yom Kippur. But where I'd always found that I didn't want to go through the process of self-reflection for God's sake, in Japan, it spoke to me. It's part of the natural order of things—as the year turns over, it makes sense to stop and think and celebrate.

I know it might seem gratuitous to include a section about New Year's in a book about living more Japanese. After all, it's not so different from how we end the year in the States with Thanksgiving, Christmas, Hanukkah, and New Year's Eve. But when I step back and think about the moments where I feel most Japanese, New Year's is right at the top. We still do all the major Jewish and American holidays in our house, but New Year's is the most important day of the Orkins' year.

Top left: Perfectly shaped ripe fruit is a popular gift in Japan.
Top right: Whole sea bream cooked in rice (tai meshi).
Bottom: Our New Year's spread, with osechi ryori and duck soba.

Simmered Chicken and Vegetables (Nimono)

Serves 4

The word *nimono* means "simmered," which pretty much sums up this classic New Year's dish: chicken and vegetables simmered slowly in seasoned dashi. I think of it like cholent, the beef stew that Jewish families make for Shabbat, when they're not supposed to work or cook from sundown Friday to sundown Saturday. You start cooking cholent on Friday and let it simmer all night long until you come back from temple on Saturday afternoon, totally famished and ready to eat.

Obviously there are no such restrictions about cooking when it comes to Japanese New Year's, but nimono functions similarly for our family. We wake up on New Year's Day, turn on the TV, and immediately begin drinking and grazing on snacks. A pot of nimono waits on the stove all day, and we help ourselves to a bowl whenever we feel like eating something a little more substantial. You can make nimono at any time of the year, but there will always be a batch in my house on January 1st.

5 dried shiitake mushrooms

2 teaspoons vegetable oil

8 ounces boneless, skinless chicken thighs, sliced into ½-inch-wide strips

8 ounces carrots, peeled and sliced on the bias into 1-inch-wide pieces

8 ounces small taro roots, peeled and sliced into ½-inch-thick rounds

8 ounces lotus root, peeled, halved lengthwise, and sliced into 1-inch-thick half-moons

4 ounces burdock root (gobo) or other hearty root vegetable, peeled and sliced into 2-inch lengths

2 cups Dashi (page 28)

⅓ cup mirin

⅓ cup soy sauce

⅓ cup sake

1 tablespoon sugar

1. Place the mushrooms in a bowl and cover with 3 cups hot water. Allow to soak for at least 15 minutes or up to an hour. (Alternatively, cover the mushrooms with 3 cups cold water and microwave them for 3 minutes instead of soaking.) After the mushrooms are reconstituted, scoop them out of the water and squeeze the excess liquid back into the bowl. Save the liquid, remove the stems, and cut the mushrooms into quarters.

2. Heat a 4-quart pot, donabe, or Dutch oven over medium heat, then coat with the vegetable oil. Add the chicken and sauté for 2 minutes. Stir in the carrots, taro, lotus root, and burdock, then cover with the dashi, mirin, soy sauce, sake, and reserved mushroom-soaking liquid. Stir in the sugar and bring to a simmer, then drop the heat as low as it will go. Partially cover with a lid, or cut a round of parchment paper with a small hole in the center and place it directly on top of the broth. Simmer very gently for 1 hour, or until all the vegetables and meat are tender. Serve.

Whole Fish Cooked in Rice (Tai Meshi)

Serves 4

Every year we try to include at least one showstopper dish in our New Year's Eve dinner. Sometimes we'll roast a prime rib or some other hunk of meat. Other years we'll make tai meshi.

Tai meshi isn't necessarily a New Year's dish, but it's one of the most festive things you can serve. You come out to the dining room with a big pot and remove the lid to unveil a whole fish steamed over rice—simultaneously elegant and badass. See it once, and you get it. And, thankfully, it's a lot less work than it seems. You sear the fish, place it in the pot, and let it cook with the rice. The fish bestows the rice with a really lovely perfume that you augment with a sprinkling of green onions and sesame seeds. Everyone oohs and aahs, and then you take it back to the kitchen to divvy into individual portions that people season to taste with salt and togarashi.

1½ cups Japanese short-grain rice

One 5-inch square kombu or
   1½ cups Dashi (page 28)

1 whole small sea bream, red
   snapper, or porgy (about
   1 pound), cleaned and scaled

2 teaspoons kosher salt

2 tablespoons soy sauce

1 tablespoon sake

1 tablespoon mirin

1 tablespoon vegetable oil

1 tablespoon roasted sesame seeds

2 negi (Japanese green onions)
   or 4 scallions, sliced very thin
   on the bias (about ½ cup)

FOR SERVING

Sea salt

Shichimi togarashi

1. Place the rice in a fine-mesh strainer and rinse under cold water, agitating the grains with your fingers to help wash off the starch, until the water runs almost clear. (Alternatively, place the rice in a pot or bowl and rinse and drain away the water three times.) Transfer the rice to a large (3- to 4-quart) donabe or similarly sized Dutch oven or heavy-bottomed pot. Add the kombu and 1¾ cups water to the pot and allow to soak for 30 minutes. Or, if you have 1½ cups of dashi at the ready, simply add it to the pot.

2. Meanwhile, prep the fish. Cut five ½-inch-deep diagonal slits into each side of the fish. Rub the salt into the slits and the cavity.

3. Remove and discard the kombu, if using. Stir in the soy sauce, sake, and mirin and allow the rice to soak for 20 more minutes.

4. Heat a large nonstick pan over high heat, then coat with the vegetable oil. Once the oil is shimmering, add the fish and sear on both sides; 2 to 3 minutes per side should be enough to give the skin some color and the fish a head start on cooking. Remove from the heat.

5. Place the seared fish on top of the rice and set the pot over high heat. If the fish is too big to lie flat, curl the tail end up around the edge of the pot, or cut off the head and set it on top of the rice next to the body. Bring the rice to a simmer, then drop the heat as low as it will go, cover the pot, and cook for 14 minutes. Shut off the heat and allow to stand, covered, for 10 minutes.

6. Uncover the pot and give your diners a peek at what's inside. Then carefully remove the fish and add the sesame seeds and negi or scallions to the pot. Use a fork or chopsticks to fluff and mix the rice. Cover again while you pick the meat from the fish. Stir the fish into the rice and serve immediately, with a dish of sea salt and another of shichimi togarashi on the side.

Duck Soba (Kamo Soba)

Serves 2 as a main dish, 4 as an appetizer

My wife and her friends will tell you that there are fewer and fewer people in Japan upholding the traditions they grew up with. They're the last generation, they say, that is abiding by things like eating a bowl of soba right at midnight on New Year's Eve. Noodles represent longevity in Japan and many other Asian countries. The buckwheat in the noodles has meaning too, as do their shape and length. Our friend Ayoko says that Japanese people eat soba on New Year's rather than udon because soba is long, while udon is thick, which speaks to Japanese people's modesty—whatever that means. Everyone has their own explanation of the meaning of New Year's food. I usually nod my head in agreement, because who am I to argue?

Toshikoshi soba (New Year's soba) is usually a pretty plain affair, but I'm not really Japanese, so I like to gussy things up a bit by making the dish with seared duck breast and a flavorful dashi-based broth. Mari says it's fine and doesn't offend her traditionalist sensibilities, which is generally all the permission I require. Nevertheless, the noodles are the star of the show here. If you live near a good Japanese market, buy the most expensive soba you can find—it's worth the splurge, especially on New Year's.

1 skin-on Pekin duck breast (about 5 ounces)

Kosher salt

4 scallions, cut into 2-inch lengths

3 cups Dashi (page 28)

3 tablespoons plus 1 teaspoon soy sauce

1 tablespoon plus 1 teaspoon mirin

7 ounces dried thick-cut soba noodles

½ cup Seasoned Spinach (Ohitashi, page 204)

1. With a sharp knife, score the skin of the duck breast diagonally every ¼ inch, being careful not to slice all the way to the meat, then repeat in the opposite direction to create a crosshatch pattern. Scoring helps render the fat and crisp the skin. Season the breast on both sides with 1 teaspoon salt and let sit at room temperature for 20 minutes.

2. Pour ¼ cup water into a medium nonstick or well-seasoned skillet and set it over medium heat. Place the duck in the pan, skin side down, and cook until the water has completely evaporated, then continue to cook until the skin is browned and crisp, about 15 minutes more. Flip the duck over and cook to medium-rare, 3 to 5 minutes. Transfer the breast to a cutting board.

3. Drain the fat from the pan, return it to medium heat, and add the scallions. Cook until lightly browned and wilted, about 2 minutes. Remove and set aside.

4. Bring 6 cups water to a boil in a medium pot and season liberally with salt. In a separate saucepan, bring the dashi, soy sauce, mirin, and 1 teaspoon salt to a simmer.

5. Cook the soba in the boiling water according to the package instructions, then drain and divide among two or four bowls. Thinly slice the duck on a diagonal. Ladle the hot broth over the noodles and top with the slices of duck and the browned scallions. Add a spoonful of ohitashi and serve immediately.

Chicken Stuffed with Burdock Root and Carrots (Toriniku no Yasai Maki)

Serves 4 as part of a larger meal

New Year's dishes (osechi ryori) can differ wildly from region to region. We're a total Tokyo family, and this dish is sophisticated while being mindful of tradition in a very Tokyo way. Slices of stuffed chicken roulade make for an elegant presentation, while the burdock root has symbolic associations with a long, stable life.

The process for stuffing, rolling, poaching, and pan-searing the chicken breast is a bit involved, but that's what the holidays are for, right? If we were an Italian family, we might make the Feast of the Seven Fishes for Christmas Eve and a timpano for New Year's. We demonstrate our love for friends and family by putting a little extra effort into dinner. And there's nothing especially difficult here—it just takes a little craftiness and confidence to do it well.

2 cups Dashi (page 28) or 1 cup tightly packed katsuobushi (bonito flakes)

1 tablespoon soy sauce

1 tablespoon mirin

1 teaspoon kosher salt

One 12-inch piece burdock root (gobo), peeled and sliced into ¼-inch-thick batons

1 medium carrot, peeled and sliced into ¼-inch-thick batons

2 boneless, skinless chicken breasts (about 8 ounces each)

½ cup all-purpose flour

2 tablespoons vegetable oil

¾ cup Tare (Seasoning Sauce, page 237), Simplified Tare (page 235), or Teriyaki 12.0 (page 61)

1. Bring the dashi to a simmer in a sauté pan. If you don't have dashi, bring 3 cups water to a bare simmer in a sauté pan, then shut off the heat, add the katsuobushi, cover, and let sit for 15 minutes. Strain through a fine-mesh strainer and return the liquid to the pan. In either case, add the soy sauce, mirin, and salt and stir to dissolve.

2. Add the burdock to the pan and cook for 5 minutes, then add the carrot and cook for 15 minutes more, or until both are tender. Remove the vegetables as they are done and dunk into an ice bath. Don't leave the vegetables in the bath for too long—pull them out once they've cooled to room temperature. (Save the poaching liquid for soup or other poaching jobs.)

3. One at a time, flatten each chicken breast to an even ½-inch thickness: Lay the breast on a cutting board. Use a sharp knife to butterfly it—slice it horizontally in half, stopping ½ inch short of slicing it all the way through. Open the breast up like a book, place it between two sheets of plastic wrap, and use a meat mallet or rolling pin to lightly pound it to an even thickness of a little more than ¼ inch.

4. One at a time, place each chicken breast on a large sheet of plastic wrap and lay a few pieces of burdock in a straight line across the meat, about 3 inches from the top. Follow with a row of carrot below the first row, another row of burdock, and one more row of carrot. Roll the meat up tightly around the vegetables and then wrap tightly in the plastic wrap, twisting the ends to tighten it and shape it into an even/smooth roulade. Wrap in two more layers of plastic and then a layer of foil.

5. Heat the oven to 250°F. Place the breasts on a rack set in a roasting pan and fill the pan with enough water to come just under the rack. Slide the whole thing into the oven and cook for 1 to 1½ hours, or until the chicken is

firm to the touch and the internal temperature is 140°F. Remove the breasts from the oven, remove the foil, and plunge them into an ice bath to stop cooking.

6. Unwrap the chicken breasts and pat them dry with paper towels.

Put the flour in a shallow container and roll the breasts in it, dusting off the excess. Heat a large skillet over medium-high heat, then coat with the vegetable oil. Add the chicken breasts and brown on all sides, 5 to 7 minutes. Pour in the tare or teriyaki sauce and cook until the

sauce is reduced to a syrupy consistency, rolling the breasts in the sauce as it simmers to coat.

7. Remove from the heat and allow to cool slightly, then cut the breasts into ½-inch-thick slices and serve immediately.

Rice Cakes (Mochi)

Makes as many as you like

Mochi was the least degenerate of the many discoveries I made in college. A classmate from Osaka introduced me to it one night in his dorm room, where he pulled a hot rice cake from his toaster oven and handed it to me wrapped in a piece of nori. Simultaneously crisp and gooey, the thing was a mindblower, and I've been nuts about mochi ever since.

Mochi are rice cakes made by pounding cooked sticky rice into a taffy-like shmoo (Chris's word). In America we most commonly see mochi in the freezer aisle, where you can buy baby-fist–size ice cream nuggets wrapped in colorful mochi. In Japan, mochi are much more common, especially in traditional confections known as *wagashi*. They're also an important part of New Year's celebrations. In Tokyo, during the last weeks of the year, I'd often come across groups of people in parks and marketplaces pounding hot rice in giant mortars. One person would reach in and turn the ball of rice, pulling his or her hand away just as another person brought a mallet down to smash the rice. It's a beautifully choreographed dance, tinged with the slight danger that someone's appendage could be crushed at any moment.

It's also a pain in the ass, so I rely on bags of kiri mochi (cut mochi) that come individually wrapped. You can find them at most Asian markets, usually in the rice aisle. They're hard as a rock when they come out of the bag but soften quickly when you heat them. You'll find all kinds of different uses for them; here I've given you three of my favorites.

Kiri mochi (hard rectangles or rounds of packaged mochi)

HEAT THE MOCHI

Mochi is like napalm when it gets hot and drippy, so be very careful. Speaking from experience here.

IN AN OVEN (OR TOASTER OVEN): Heat the oven to 425°F. Lay the mochi on a baking sheet—or directly on the oven rack, if it won't slip through—and bake until the mochi puffs up and begins to turn golden, usually 5 to 8 minutes. (At home I use my toaster oven; I just slide the mochi in and set it to toast.) Remove carefully.

ON A GRILL RACK SET OVER A LOW FLAME: If you happen to have a small wire grate that fits over your gas range, you can grill a piece of mochi for about 2 minutes over very low heat, flipping it often, until it puffs up and begins to turn golden. Remove carefully.

IN A MICROWAVE: This is not the most desirable method because you won't get any crispness, but if you gotta have your mochi in a hurry, place it on a heatproof plate and microwave for about 20 seconds on high power, until it puffs and softens.

ACCOUTREMENTS

Pick one route, or throw a choose-your-own-mochi party by setting out the various options. All of these ingredients are readily available at Japanese markets and online.

FILLED WITH SWEET RED BEAN PASTE: Place a warm piece of mochi on a cutting board and use a spatula (or your palm, if you're feeling daring) to smash it flat. Place 1 tablespoon sweet red bean paste (anko) in the center of the mochi and wrap the mochi around it. Use your fingers to seal the cake, and enjoy.

RECIPE CONTINUES

NEW YEAR'S

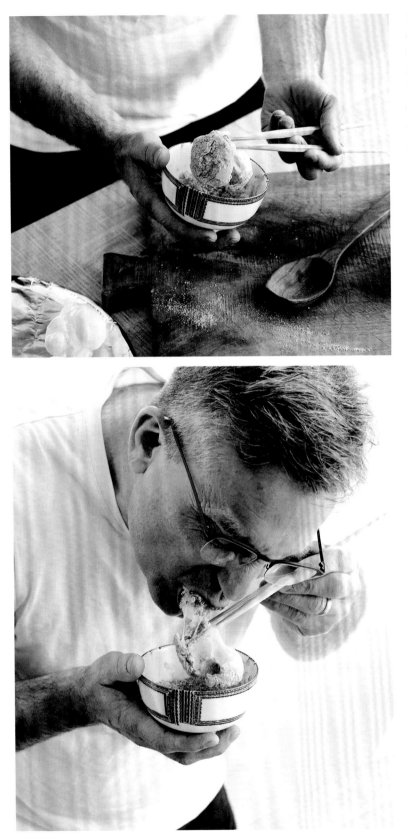

DUSTED WITH KINAKO (TOASTED SOY FLOUR): For each piece, mix together 1 tablespoon kinako and 2 teaspoons sugar in a small bowl. Use a pair of chopsticks to dunk a warm piece of mochi into a cup or bowl of warm water, then immediately drop the mochi into the kinako mixture. Stir it around to coat, then gobble it up.

WRAPPED IN NORI AND DIPPED IN SOY SAUCE: For each piece, mix together 2 tablespoons soy sauce and 1 tablespoon mirin in a small bowl. Wrap a piece of warm mochi in a quarter sheet of nori and dip it into the sauce as you eat. (If you like, you can toast the nori over an open flame first.)

JUBAKO

Jubako are one of the loveliest parts of Japanese New Year's. They're stackable, ornate lacquered-wood boxes that you fill with various symbolic foods—called *osechi ryori*—for your guests to snack on while they sip booze and beer: sweetened black beans, candied anchovies, rolled omelets, poached prawns, and other tasty morsels. Each item is tucked neatly into a compartment of the jubako box to create an assortment that's almost too pretty to eat. Almost.

Sadly, I've noticed the tradition in decline over the past twenty or so years. About a decade ago, Mari and I bought a gorgeous three-tier jubako, and we started filling it with homemade osechi ryori every year for New Year's. You don't have to do the same thing, but you should absolutely give the snacks in the following section a whirl. They're all delicious and perfectly suited for nibbling on throughout the day, New Year's or otherwise.

Sweet Dashi-Poached Prawns (Ebi no Umani)

Serves 5 as part of a larger meal

Simmered, marinated prawns are a perennial part of a jubako box as a symbol of long life. I guess their curved bodies are reminiscent of an elderly person's hunched back, but I like to straighten them out with skewers before cooking. Any large shrimp will do, but most of the other typical dishes in a jubako are small and/or vegetarian, and a big head-on prawn comes across as especially luxurious and substantial. If you live in a place where you can purchase fresh head-on spot prawns, do it.

One 5-inch square kombu

5 large prawns, preferably head-on, or large shrimp

½ cup soy sauce

¼ cup mirin

¼ cup sake

2 tablespoons sugar

½ cup tightly packed katsuobushi (bonito flakes)

1 tablespoon plus 2 teaspoons kosher salt

EQUIPMENT

5 wooden skewers, cut to the same length as the prawns

1. Place the kombu in a medium saucepan, add 4 cups cold water, and let soak for 30 minutes to 1 hour.

2. Meanwhile, devein the prawns (or shrimp) without peeling them: Insert a toothpick close to the prawn's back, between two segments of shell, and use it to pull out the dark vein that runs down the length of each prawn. If you don't get all of it in one go, repeat the process as necessary, moving along the prawn's back to another segment of shell. (If you've never done this before, this is what the internet was made for.) Next, push a skewer into each prawn, starting at the tail and running to the head to prevent them from curling during cooking.

3. From here, you're going to poach the shrimp quickly and then immediately cover them in warm tare. This will be pretty straightforward if you have everything ready to go. First, prepare the tare: Combine the soy sauce, mirin, sake, and sugar in a small saucepan over medium heat and bring to a simmer, stirring to dissolve the sugar. Remove from the heat and add the katsuobushi.

4. Bring the soaked kombu and water to a simmer over medium heat. Add the salt and stir to dissolve. Lower in the prawns and poach them for 2 minutes.

5. Transfer the prawns to a flat-bottomed container that holds them snugly. If the tare has cooled significantly, bring it back to a simmer, then pour it over the prawns. Lay a paper towel directly on the prawns. The towel will soak up the sauce and ensure that they're fully covered. Let cool to room temperature, then serve, with a bowl on the side for the shells.

Mashed Sweet Potatoes
with Candied Chestnuts (Kuri Kinton)

Serves 4 to 6 as a snack

Kuri kinton is a bit difficult to describe to the uninitiated, because it doesn't have a lot of Western analogues. You don't see a mix of textures like this very often in American cooking—creamy-chewy chestnuts nestled in a thick mash of sweet potatoes—and we're not very accustomed to having sweet dishes side by side with salty ones. But it's a requisite part of a New Year's spread, and I've come to love it. The orange-yellow color is intended to be reminiscent of gold, and the dish is a symbol of good financial fortune.

To make kuri kinton, you'll need jarred chestnuts in syrup (kuri kanroni), which are available online if you don't have a Japanese market nearby. They're often tinted with gardenia pods (or food coloring), which give the syrup a yellow hue. If you can find gardenia pods (online or at a Chinese herb store), add them to the mix to give the dish an even—excuse the pun—richer hue.

1 pound sweet potatoes, preferably Japanese, peeled

4 gardenia pods (optional; see headnote)

¾ cup sugar

2 tablespoons mirin

1 teaspoon kosher salt

10 jarred chestnuts in syrup (kuri kanroni), sliced in half, plus 2 tablespoons of their syrup

1. Slice the potatoes into ½-inch-thick rounds, place in a medium pot, and cover with water by 1 inch. If you've managed to find gardenia pods, add them to the pot. Bring to a bare simmer over high heat, then drop the heat to low and cook until the potatoes are very soft, 20 to 25 minutes.

2. Drain the potatoes in a colander; discard the gardenia pods, if you used them. If you have a potato ricer or food mill, pass the potatoes through the finest holes. If not, use a sturdy rubber spatula to press the potatoes through a fine-mesh strainer. Or, if you have nothing else, use a potato masher—they won't be as smooth, but that's okay.

3. Combine the potatoes and sugar in a large nonstick skillet set over medium heat and heat until the potatoes begin to sizzle lightly, then cook, stirring constantly, for 3 minutes. Add the mirin, salt, and the reserved 2 tablespoons chestnut syrup and cook and stir for 4 minutes. Finally, stir in the chestnuts and cook for 1 more minute. Transfer to a baking sheet and spread out in an even layer to cool. (You can store the remaining kuri kinton in the fridge for up to a couple days.) Serve at room temperature.

Sweet Black Soybeans (Kuromame)

Serves 4 to 6 as a snack

I love these—they're so beautiful, like shiny black gems you can pop in your mouth. None of my Japanese family loves them as much as I do, but I even buy them out of season from the department store market (depachika) whenever I see them. They take a long time to cook, but not having a dish of these sweet morsels on New Year's is like a Seder plate without the lamb bone: sacrilege. They're also incredible stuffed into warm Mochi (page 219) or spooned with a little of their syrup over vanilla ice cream.

1½ cups (9 ounces) dried black soybeans, rinsed and picked over
1⅓ cups sugar
½ teaspoon baking powder
½ teaspoon salt
3 tablespoons soy sauce

1. Combine all the ingredients in a saucepan with 4 cups water. Bring to a simmer over medium heat, stirring to dissolve the dry ingredients and skimming any unsightly foam that rises to the surface. Once it reaches a simmer, add ½ cup cold water and bring to a simmer again. Turn off the heat, cover, and allow to soak for at least 5 hours or overnight.

2. From here, you have two options for cooking the beans. If you have a pressure cooker, I highly recommend using it. If not, you can cook the beans slowly on the stove.

TRADITIONAL STOVETOP: Bring the beans and liquid to a simmer over medium-high heat, then drop the heat to low and simmer gently for 4 to 6 hours, adding water whenever necessary to keep the beans covered. The beans are done when they're tender and easily smushed.

IN A PRESSURE COOKER: Bring the beans and liquid to a simmer over medium-high heat, then add them to a pressure cooker. Seal and cook under high pressure for 20 minutes, then shut off the heat and allow the pressure to release naturally.

3. Strain the beans (reserving the liquid) and set aside to cool. Transfer the cooking liquid to a saucepan and simmer over medium-high heat for 30 minutes, or until the liquid has reduced to a syrupy consistency. Let the syrup cool slightly, then mix together with the beans. Serve at room temperature, or cover and refrigerate for up to a few days.

Sweet Rolled Omelet
with Fish Cake (Datemaki)

Serves 4 to 6 as a snack

This is a fluffier, fancier version of tamagoyaki, the sweet-savory omelet you see at sushi bars or in our Giant Sushi (Futomaki, page 200). Where a regular tamagoyaki is a celebration of the pure taste of egg—maybe with the addition of smokiness from dashi—datemaki takes things to a sweeter, fishier place. For starters, the egg mixture is made with pieces of hanpen—pillowy fish cakes that both flavor the omelet and give it extra volume. Then, rather than trying to keep the omelet pale and barely cooked, you let datemaki sit in the pan until browned on one side, so that when you roll it up and slice it, the slices have a beautiful visible spiral in the center.

There are special bamboo mats with deep grooves in them that will give datemaki its signature gear-like appearance, but you can use whatever rolling mat you have, or even just a piece of plastic wrap. And don't beat yourself up if your maiden attempt doesn't look perfect. It'll still taste delicious, and I guarantee your second try will be better than your first.

8 ounces hanpen (spongy
  fish cakes)

6 large eggs, beaten

3 tablespoons sugar

1 tablespoon mirin

1 tablespoon sake

1 tablespoon vegetable oil
  (or cooking spray)

1. Dice the hanpen into ¼-inch pieces and transfer to a bowl, along with the eggs. Add the sugar, mirin, and sake, then use a hand-held blender to puree thoroughly. You can do this with a standard blender, but you'll end up whipping in more air, so you'll need to let the mixture settle for a couple minutes before proceeding. Pass the egg mixture through a strainer into a bowl and set aside.

2. If you have a bamboo sushi mat, lay it flat on a cutting board and cover with a piece of plastic wrap. If not, just a large piece of plastic wrap will do.

3. Set a 12-inch nonstick skillet over low heat and coat with the oil (or cooking spray). Pour the egg mixture into the pan and stir gently and constantly with a rubber spatula until the eggs begin to set. Stop stirring and let the omelet cook until the bottom is nicely browned and the top is nearly cooked through, about 15 minutes. If the omelet sets before the bottom browns, turn the heat up to get some color on there.

4. Slide the omelet onto the plastic wrap. Use the wrap to lift one side of the omelet and begin rolling it into a cylinder; pull the plastic wrap away as you go, so it doesn't end up wrapped in the omelet. If the eggs are too firm to roll, use a sharp knife to score shallow parallel lines in the omelet every ½ inch or so to help it roll more easily.

5. Remove the plastic and place the omelet in the center of the bamboo mat. (If you don't have a bamboo mat, leave the omelet wrapped in the plastic as it cools. It won't be as tight or pretty, but that's okay.) Roll the mat up around the omelet, squeezing it a bit tighter this time, then secure with rubber bands or a piece of string and allow to cool to room temperature.

6. Once it's cooled, unwrap the omelet, slice into ½-inch-thick slices, and serve.

Candied Sardines (Tazukuri)

Serves 4 to 6 as a snack

These little suckers are another tough sell for some Americans, but they shouldn't be. They're chewy like candied fruit peel, sweet, and packed with umami. I might not be able to convince you to eat sweet whole tiny fish as a snack, but I can tell you that there are few things that go better with a cold beer.

1 ounce dried baby sardines (niboshi)
2 tablespoons sake
2 tablespoons mirin
2 tablespoons soy sauce
2 tablespoons sugar

1. Heat a small saucepan over low heat, then add the sardines and toast the fish, stirring constantly, until fragrant, about 4 minutes. Remove the fish from the pan and set aside.

2. Add the sake, mirin, soy sauce, sugar, and 2 tablespoons water to the pan and stir to dissolve the sugar, then return the sardines to the pan. Simmer over very low heat, stirring frequently, until most of the liquid has evaporated or been absorbed, about 10 minutes.

3. Spread the sardines out on a lightly greased or parchment-lined cookie sheet and allow to cool. Once completely cooled, they'll keep in an airtight container for a couple days.

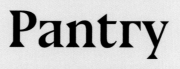

Pantry

Pickled Garlic

Makes 1½ cups

At Ivan Ramen, we mix slivers of pickled garlic into our richer noodle dishes for a little burst of tart piquancy. The salty/sour/sweet pickling liquid is also a great seasoning on its own. This is best made at least 2 days before you intend to use it, and it'll keep in the fridge for at least a month. Vegetarians can omit the katsuobushi.

8 ounces garlic, peeled
⅔ cup soy sauce
⅔ cup white vinegar
7 tablespoons sugar
¼ cup tightly packed katsuobushi
  (bonito flakes; optional)

1. Thinly slice the garlic, either by hand or by using a slicing blade on a food processor.

2. Bring 6 cups water to a simmer in a saucepan. Add the sliced garlic and simmer for 5 minutes. Drain and transfer to a small mason jar or other heatproof container.

3. Combine the soy sauce, vinegar, and sugar in a saucepan and bring to a simmer over medium heat, stirring to dissolve the sugar. Add the katsuobushi, if using. Allow to steep for 5 minutes, then strain the hot brine and pour over the garlic. Allow to cool.

4. Cover the garlic and refrigerate overnight before using. The pickled garlic will keep in the fridge for weeks.

Satsuma Vinegar (or Liqueur)

Makes about 4 cups

In Japan, when the ume (Japanese green plums) came into season every June, my industrious friends would busy themselves making various plum-related products. My neighbor would make a batch of umeboshi (the salted fermented plums used in some of the recipes in this book), and I would set about the easier task of making umeshu (plum liqueur) and umesu (plum vinegar).

Both umeshu and umesu are made the same way, with three ingredients: ume, rock sugar, and vinegar or clear liquor. A few liters of umeshu would last me all year, but I'd make gallons of plum vinegar to season my cold summer ramen. The saddest day of summer was always when I ran out of the vinegar and knew that I had to wait until the following June to have it again. But what a Japanese feeling to have! Being sad about the fleeting nature of a seasonal treat was how I knew I was adapting to my new home in a real and meaningful way.

Finding Japanese green plums (they're actually a variety of apricot) in the States is difficult, so these recipes for vinegar and liqueur call for satsumas, a type of mandarin orange. If you want to experiment with other fruit, the basic formula is the same: Layer equal amounts of fruit and rock sugar in a jar and cover with an equal weight of white vinegar or liquor: e.g., 1 pound fruit, 1 pound rock sugar, and 4 cups liquor or vinegar. You can use any good-quality grain alcohol or vodka, but you want it to have as clean a flavor as possible.

Note: If you're lucky enough to have a source for ume, wash them vigorously under cold water and dry them well. Use a toothpick to pull out the dried eye of the stem at the top of each plum and proceed as directed.

1 pound white rock sugar
(available in Asian markets)
1 pound satsuma oranges
(or another variety of mandarins
or tangerines), sliced into
quarters
4 cups rice vinegar (for the
vinegar) or shochu or vodka
(for the liqueur)

1. Spread a layer of rock sugar in a glass jar or other tall nonreactive container, then gently lay a few satsuma quarters onto the sugar. Repeat until you've used all the sugar and fruit.

2. Cover with the rice vinegar or alcohol, seal the jar, and refrigerate for 1 week, giving the container a shake once a day. Strain the vinegar or liqueur and store in the fridge for up to a few months.

Chunky Chili Oil (Taberu Rayu)

Makes about 3 cups

Taberu rayu is a spicy oil you can—almost—eat by the spoonful. It was all the rage in Japan when we last lived in Tokyo, and it's become a staple on our table at home. It's gloriously simple to make—you can probably pull it together with ingredients that are in the pantry of your parents' suburban house, or at least the local grocery store.

The only wild card in the recipe is the chile. If you're unsure of the spice level of various dried chiles, you'll have to gamble and pick one. Tried-and-true crushed red pepper flakes work fine too, if that's all you can get.

Oh, and by the way, jars of this stuff make amazing gifts.

2 cups neutral-flavored oil (grapeseed or vegetable work well)

½ cup crushed dried red chiles of your choice (or red pepper flakes)

¼ cup unsalted roasted almonds, crushed or chopped into small pieces

¼ cup roasted sesame seeds

¼ cup fried or dried onions (store-bought)

3 tablespoons fried or dried garlic (store-bought or homemade)

2 tablespoons soy sauce

1 tablespoon sugar

1 teaspoon kosher salt

Stir together the oil and chiles (or red pepper flakes) and bring to a gentle simmer in a small saucepan over medium-low heat. Stir in the remaining ingredients, return to a low simmer, and cook for 3 minutes, then remove from the heat. The oil is ready to use as soon as it's cooled to room temperature, but it'll only improve after a day or two. Transfer to a glass or plastic container, seal, and store in the fridge for up to 2 weeks. Give it a good shake or stir before serving.

Tare (Seasoning Sauce)

Makes 2 cups

To me, this is the ideal multipurpose barbecue sauce. It's both sweet and umami, and it gets even better when it's caramelized on a hot grill. Brush it on any kind of yakitori—chicken, beef, pork, fish, or vegetable.

1 cup soy sauce

⅔ cup Dashi (page 28)

⅓ cup mirin

3 tablespoons plus 1 teaspoon sake

¼ cup sugar

2 tablespoons honey

Combine all of the ingredients in a small saucepan and bring to a boil over medium-high heat, then lower the heat to a simmer and cook for 5 minutes, stirring to make sure the sugar is fully dissolved. Cool to room temperature, then store in an airtight container in the fridge. This is best if used within a week, but it'll keep for a couple weeks.

Simplified Tare

Makes ¾ cup

This is a simplified tare you can use to marinate or brush onto meat, or you can reduce it to a glaze in a pan and paint onto whatever you like.

¼ cup soy sauce

¼ cup sake

¼ cup mirin

1 tablespoon sugar

Combine all the ingredients in a bowl and whisk to dissolve the sugar. Transfer to a jar and store in the fridge for up to a month. Give it a shake or stir before using.

Sesame Furikake (Rice Topping)

Makes 1 cup

This is the most common variety of furikake, which is usually used as a rice topping, but you should feel just as free to sprinkle it over steamed vegetables, stir-fries, oatmeal, or popcorn. One of the most successful applications we've ever come up with for it is on top of Smoked Fish Donburi (page 97). Turns out furikake and smoked fish are a perfect fit. Your bagels and lox will never be the same.

½ cup dried onion flakes

½ cup aonori (powdered dried green seaweed)

2 tablespoons plus 1 teaspoon white sesame seeds

2 tablespoons plus 1 teaspoon black sesame seeds

1 tablespoon sugar

1 teaspoon kosher salt

Pulse the dried onion in a food processor or spice grinder five times, or until powdery. Transfer to a bowl, add the remaining ingredients, and stir well. Store in an airtight container for up to a couple weeks. Give it a good shake before serving.

Katsuobushi Furikake

Makes about 1½ cups

Furikake is endlessly useful as a topping. (I think my cooks at the restaurants rely on it too much, to be honest.) This version works really well with the Miso-Buttered Corn (page 93), but I'm sure you'll find all kinds of other rewarding places to sprinkle it.

2 cups tightly packed katsuobushi (bonito flakes)

⅓ cup white sesame seeds

⅓ cup black sesame seeds

1 tablespoon plus 1 teaspoon togarashi shichimi

1 tablespoon kosher salt

Working in batches, use a mortar and pestle, food processor, or spice grinder to pulverize the katsuobushi flakes into a fine powder. Transfer to a bowl, add the remaining ingredients, and stir well. Store in an airtight container for up to a week.

Ingredients

Believe me, I find it just as frustrating as you do when I open a cookbook and find that I need to buy an entire cupboard's worth of obscure ingredients that I'll never use again. I've tried my best to make the recipes in this book accessible to everyone, regardless of whether you live near a great Japanese market or not. The internet has certainly made it easier for people stuck in a culinary wasteland to cook delicious food, but I still don't want you to have to wait for a delivery in the mail to make dinner. The truth is, you can get through the majority of this book with ingredients you'll find at any large American grocery store or with just one online order.

If you do live in a city blessed with different Asian markets, note that you'll find vastly different items in stock depending on what kind of market it is. For this book, you're going to have the best luck shopping at Japanese markets, of course, followed by Korean, Chinese, and, finally, Southeast Asian (Vietnamese, Thai, or Lao) shops.

What follows is an overview of all the ingredients in the book that you might be unfamiliar with—what they are, where to find them, and how they're used. Please don't be worried by the length of this list; many of these items appear in only a few of the recipes, and they're often optional.

ABURA-AGE: Thin slices of tofu fried until they're golden brown and chewy. They resemble pieces of tofu skin, if you're familiar with that, but they're a different product. Abura-age are most commonly used to make Inari Sushi (Stuffed Tofu Pouches, page 55): After being simmered in sweetened soy sauce, each one is opened up to form a pouch and filled with sushi rice. You'll find packages of abura-age in the refrigerated section of the market, where you may also encounter presimmered abura-age, meant for making inari.

AONORI: Powdered dried green seaweed that brings a nice ocean flavor to a dish when sprinkled over it as a garnish. It's available in bags or small glass jars at most Asian markets.

BULL-DOG TONKATSU SAUCE: A fruity, tangy, syrupy condiment that looks like barbecue sauce. As the name implies, it's usually used as a pleasantly sweet-and-sour accompaniment to Tonkatsu (Fried Pork Cutlets, page 44) or Okonomiyaki (Savory Pancakes, page 185), but I find myself reaching for it constantly.

BURDOCK ROOT (GOBO): Long, slender roots that look like thin horseradish. They need to be peeled and washed thoroughly to remove any dirt and then cooked for a long time to soften. Gobo has a sweet, lightly medicinal flavor that's reminiscent of ginseng. If you can't find gobo, substitute your favorite hearty root vegetable: carrots, parsnips, sunchokes, or celery root.

CHIKUWA: Cylindrical brown-and-white fish cakes made light and fluffy with the addition of egg white. They have a bouncy bite and mild flavor. Find them in packages in the refrigerated aisle. Simmer them in dashi as part of an Oden Party (page 146).

CHRYSANTHEMUM GREENS: Crunchy, herbaceous, slightly bitter member of the daisy family. They look like heartier carrot tops, and they take especially well to quick steaming or frying. If you can't find chrysanthemum greens, substitute dandelion greens, broccoli rabe, or mustard greens (you'll have to adjust the cooking time accordingly).

FUKUJIN PICKLES (FUKUJINZUKE): Ruby-red pickles served alongside a bowl of Japanese curry. Fukujinzuke are usually made from a medley of chopped vegetables, such as daikon, eggplant, green beans, bamboo shoots, and lotus root. They're sweet and not too sour, a perfect foil for the richness of curry. Buy them in cans or refrigerated bags. Pickled sushi ginger makes a decent substitute.

FURIKAKE: A seasoning mixture usually made from sesame seeds, katsuobushi (bonito flakes), seaweed, sugar, and various dried herbs. There are numerous varieties of furikake and an incredibly wide range of uses, from rice topping to garnish for corn on the cob. There are two recipes for furikake in this book (pages 236 and 237), but you can find it in jars at most Asian markets.

GARLIC CHIVES (NIRA): Mild, oniony greens that resemble long blades of grass. When cooked properly, nira retain a nice bit of crunch. They're used in a number of different cuisines, so they're pretty common in Asian grocery stores, but there isn't really a great substitute. Leeks, maybe, but that's kind of a stretch.

GYOZA WRAPPERS: Thin rounds of dumpling dough made from wheat flour. The thinner, the better, I say. You can find packaged gyoza wrappers in the refrigerated section of Asian (and some standard) grocery stores.

HANPEN: Fish cakes that look like square white pillows. Like most fish cakes, hanpen are made from surimi (fish paste, usually pollock). They're found in the refrigerated section. They have very little flavor

of their own but absorb liquid well, which is why we simmer them in dashi for Oden (page 146).

IKURA: Salmon roe that's been lightly cured in soy sauce and sake. The translucent orange-red eggs are about the size of small pearls and burst open when bitten into. Good ikura has a delightful briny sweetness and an enjoyable fishiness.

JAPANESE SAUSAGES (ARABIKI SAUSAGES): Coarsely ground smoked pork sausages with snappy casings. They're a little bigger than cocktail sausages and come fully cooked.

KARASHI: Very spicy Japanese mustard. This stuff will make your sinuses sting and your eyes water, but it's totally worth it. It comes in tubes or as a powder you mix into a paste with water. Karashi turns up only once in this book, as an accompaniment to Oden (page 146).

KATSUOBUSHI: Thinly shaved flakes of smoked dried bonito. This is one of the building blocks of Japanese cuisine and one of the two ingredients in Dashi (page 28). It brings an inimitable smoky umami flavor to whatever party it joins, and it appears over and over again in this book, often steeped in various sauces and soups. I also like to chop it fine and sprinkle it over Clay Pot Mixed Rice (Takikomi Gohan, page 116). You'll find it in bags, usually near the dried seaweed.

KEWPIE MAYO: A beloved brand of Japanese mayonnaise that's a little thinner and creamier than its American counterpart. It's also tangier and packed with umami, thanks to a dose of MSG. It comes in odd vase-shaped tubes decorated with a drawing of a naked baby.

KINAKO: Finely ground roasted soybean flour that has a nutty flavor and coats like powdered sugar. You can take kinako in either a savory or sweet direction by adding salt or sugar. It's one of my favorite toppings for Mochi (Rice Cakes; page 219).

KIRI MOCHI: Precut rectangles of mochi (pounded rice cakes) that come individually wrapped in bags. Kiri mochi are rock-hard when they come out of the wrapper and need to be softened through cooking, either in the oven (or a toaster oven) or on the grill. (You can also find packaged disks of mochi—kagami mochi—that function identically to kiri mochi.)

KOMBU: Dried kelp used to season dashi and other broths. Steeping a piece of kombu in liquid for an hour or so adds both umami and a touch of sea flavor. There's a wide range of kombu types and quality levels. Suffice it to say, you're looking for flattened sheets of dried seaweed that are usually coated in a thin layer of powdery sea salt. Use scissors or kitchen shears to cut the kombu into the size you need.

KOMBU MAKI: Adorable rolls of dried seaweed that are tied up with strings of dried edible gourd. Kombu maki need to be simmered to soften them, which makes them ideal for Oden (page 146).

KURI KANRONI: Chestnuts soaked in sugar syrup. These are usually mixed with cooked sweet potato and served at New Year's (page 224). Available in jars at Japanese markets and online.

LOTUS ROOT: The long tubular stems (rhizomes, technically) of lotus plants that grow underwater or in the mud. You'll find sections of lotus root sold in many Asian markets. They're usually about 2 inches in diameter and 4 to 6 inches long, with a thin but tough brown skin that needs to be peeled before cooking. A cross section of lotus root has a snowflake-like pattern that's pretty beautiful, and the flesh of the root is starchy-crunchy and mildly sweet. If you can't find lotus root, water chestnuts or sunchokes make a decent substitute in cooked preparations. Pickled daikon can step in for pickled lotus root.

MENTAIKO: Cured, seasoned cod or pollock roe that has a flavor reminiscent of bottarga and a texture like the flying-fish roe you see on sushi. Mentaiko comes in squishy pink-orange skeins that need to be sliced open and scraped to release the tiny eggs within. You'll find spicy and mild varieties of packaged mentaiko in the refrigerated section of Japanese or Korean markets. (Fresh unseasoned roe is called *tarako*.)

MILK BREAD (SHOKUPAN): Fluffy, slightly sweet white sandwich bread that's not unlike Wonder Bread, although the texture is a little bit chewier. Shokupan is hard to come by if you don't have access to a Japanese or Korean market (or a hip local bakery), but any white sandwich bread will make a suitable substitute.

MIRIN: Sweet rice wine that's ubiquitous in Japanese cuisine. It has a flavor similar to sake but is sweeter. Real, honest-to-god mirin is fermented from rice, giving it nuanced sweetness, umami, and complexity of flavor. What you're more likely to find at your local grocery store is aji-mirin, which is an approximation of mirin made from sugar and alcohol. It's not ideal, but it'll do in a pinch. If you can't find any kind of mirin, try substituting equal parts sake and sugar.

MISO: A fermented paste made from soybeans and barley or rice that has been inoculated with the mold *Aspergillus oryzae*. Miso is one of the most delicious and useful food products in the world. You probably know it from miso soup, but it has a rich and storied history that dates back to ancient China. Different varieties have completely different flavor profiles that range from salty and deeply savory (red/*aka*) to sweet and mild (white/*shiro*). You'll most commonly encounter a blended (*awase*) miso, which is fine for most of the recipes in this book.

MYOGA: Sweet, crunchy Japanese ginger that tastes like a cross between ordinary ginger and shallots and makes a really excellent temaki filling (page 67). Myoga resemble torpedo onions, but they're pretty rare, even in Asian grocery stores. Don't worry if you can't find them. They're totally optional and only appear once in the book.

NATTO: Absurdly sticky, very pungent fermented soybeans. You can find natto in the refrigerated section of Japanese grocery stores, where it comes in small Styrofoam boxes bundled with tiny packets of mustard and soy-dashi seasoning. See Natto, page 49, for a lengthier discussion.

NEGI: Japanese green onions that can grow to several feet in length and about an inch in diameter but have a milder bite than your everyday scallions. As with scallions, the white parts are better for cooking than the greens, but both make superb garnishes. If you can't find negi, scallions will do as a substitute.

NIBOSHI: Dried baby sardines often used in making dashi. We cook them in sugar for a chewy-fishy snack that's part of a traditional New Year's Jubako (see page 228). They're usually sold in bags, found in the same aisle as katsuobushi (bonito flakes).

NORI: Edible seaweed, as in the papery dark-green sheets you see at the sushi bar. Like kombu, there are a lot of different grades of nori. My best suggestion is that you try a few brands and settle on one you like, but avoid the snack-size squares of edible

seaweed that are often coated with oil and salt and too brittle to use as a wrap. Store nori in an airtight container and give the sheets a quick toast over an open flame before using. (A couple recipes in this book call for shredded nori, which is sold in bags or small plastic tubs.)

PANKO: Japanese bread crumbs (or, more accurately, bread *flakes*) that are lighter, crisper, and more feathery than American bread crumbs. Panko is widely available, even in American supermarkets, but if you can't find it, homemade or store-bought plain dried bread crumbs will suffice.

PONZU: A tart and savory dipping sauce, traditionally made from Japanese citrus juice—yuzu or sudachi lime, usually—vinegar, mirin, and katsuobushi (bonito flakes). It's almost always mixed with soy sauce before serving. You can find ponzu (premixed with soy) at any well-stocked supermarket, and definitely at any Asian market.

RAMEN NOODLES: It's difficult to summarize something that's been an obsession of mine for more than a decade, but at their core, ramen noodles are a wheat pasta made with the addition of an alkaline ingredient (sodium carbonate) that gives them their signature chewiness. There are a fair number of brands of fresh ramen out there these days, and you'll have to poke around to find one you like. If you live in a big city, you may come across refrigerated packages from Sun Noodle, which is my favorite commercial ramen producer.

RAYU (SOMETIMES LAYU): Chili-infused oil. This scarlet-red manna from heaven comes in small bottles at Japanese grocery stores. If you can't find it, substitute another chili oil or hot sauce. Or make the recipe for Chunky Chili Oil (Taberu Rayu) on page 234.

SAKE: Rice wine. The cheap stuff, like Sho Chiku Bai, will do for any of the recipes in this book.

SAKURA EBI: Small dried pink shrimp that are great as a crunchy, salty rice topping or filling for Giant

Sushi (Futomaki, page 200). They're usually sold in bags and can be found in the same aisle as katsuobushi (bonito flakes).

SANSHO PEPPER: A ground spice from the berries of a Japanese pepper plant. Sansho pepper has a strong citrus flavor and the same tingly-numbing sensation as Sichuan peppercorns. It shows up traditionally as a seasoning for eel and in the spice mixture shichimi togarashi.

SATSUMA-AGE: Bronze-brown fried fish cakes that are always part of my Oden Party setup (page 146). In Japan you can buy fresh, incredibly tasty satsuma-age and other fish cakes at the market, but in the States you're most likely going to have to resort to the packaged refrigerated version.

SHICHIMI TOGARASHI: A blend of ground and whole spices and aromatics (dried chiles, sansho pepper, dried orange peel, sesame seeds, ginger, nori, and shiso). This has some spicy heat and a bright, citrusy pop that is hard to replicate. There are recipes for homemade shichimi out there if you can't find it, but you should probably just buy it, online if necessary.

SHIMEJI MUSHROOMS: Slender, tender beech mushrooms that come in brown and white varieties. They're nutty and savory and take well to quick cooking. If you can't find shimejis, substitute a soft, succulent variety like shiitakes or oysters.

SHIO KOMBU: Short, thin shreds of seaweed that are simmered in soy sauce, sugar, and rice wine and then dried. It's usually used as a rice topping, but once you taste its intense sweet-salty-tangy deliciousness, you may want to add a pinch to almost everything. I adore this stuff and stock up on my favorite brand whenever I'm in Japan. You can find it in jars or bags at Japanese markets and online.

SHIRATAKI NOODLES: Squiggly, chewy, translucent-white noodles made from yam. Shirataki are becoming more and more common in American grocery stores (partly because they're gluten-free), where they're sold in liquid-filled bags at room temperature. I usually give the noodles a rinse under boiling water to wash away their odor, after which they're totally mild.

SHIRO SHOYU: Literally "white soy sauce," but don't expect the Crystal Pepsi version of soy sauce. It's still dark amber in color, but with a fruitier flavor than regular soy sauce. Shiro shoyu is a bit of a specialty item that you're likely going to have to source from the internet; it appears only once in this cookbook.

SHISO: My favorite herb. It comes in both red and green varieties and has a citrusy mint flavor and sweet licorice-y fragrance. It's difficult to come up with a one-for-one substitute (other than its cousin, perilla), but you could try a blend of cilantro, mint, and maybe a little basil. Kitazawa Seed Company is a good source for the seeds (*kitazawaseed.com*).

SHOCHU: Clear, clean-tasting liquor distilled from barley, sweet potatoes, rice, buckwheat, or brown sugar. It's stronger than sake but weaker than other hard spirits like vodka. Korean soju can be substituted.

SICHUAN PEPPERCORNS: A distinctive spice with a citrusy, floral flavor and less of the overt heat of other peppercorns. Its most distinctive feature is a tingly-numbing sensation that is commonly used in Chinese cooking to counterbalance the heat of chile spice. Due to the growing popularity of Sichuan cuisine in America, whole Sichuan peppercorns are becoming more and more common in grocery stores here.

SOY SAUCE (SHOYU): Arguably the world's most popular sauce, soy sauce is made by fermenting soybeans with either wheat or barley. It originated in China, where it was originally a by-product of fermented bean pastes, but it took on a life of its own in Japan. I vastly prefer Japanese soy sauce (shoyu) to any other version, but you can make do with what's available. Note, however, that you really do get what you pay for with soy sauce. Cheaper versions are made by taking shortcuts that lose the complexity and flavor nuances generated by long, slow fermentation.

SUSHI GINGER (GARI): Sweet vinegar-pickled young ginger, usually served in thin slices. Most people know gari from the sushi bar, although the signature pink coloring isn't always present.

SWEET RED BEAN PASTE (ANKO): A thick mash of sugar-sweetened adzuki beans that's a staple of Japanese desserts. Red bean paste, which comes in both coarse and smooth varieties, can be purchased in cans or plastic bags at various Asian grocery stores.

TAKUAN: Super-pungent bright-yellow daikon pickles often sold in long, uncut pieces or presliced in bags in the refrigerated section of Asian grocery stores. Takuan has a strong odor but doesn't taste nearly as strong as the smell would indicate. It's sweet and crunchy, with the funky savoriness of raw radishes but none of the bitterness.

TARO: Technically the corm, or underground stem, of the taro plant, although it looks like a tuber or a root. You'll see taro in a couple different forms at Asian markets. There are smooth-skinned ones and fuzzier ones; some have a speckled light-violet flesh, while others are whiter inside. In any case, think of taro as a very starchy, slightly nutty-tasting potato.

UDON: Wheat-flour noodles that vary in thickness from that of wide linguine to a toddler's finger. Udon has a pleasant bite but is less chewy than soba or ramen. You can buy udon fresh, frozen, or dried, depending on how you intend to use it.

UMEBOSHI: Fermented plums that are used in a host of different ways. The flesh of umeboshi has a soft texture, like overripe fruit. They're mouth-puckering, a little savory, salty, and fruity, with just enough residual sweetness to balance it all out. Find them in the refrigerated section of Japanese markets, and spring for the nicest ones they have. The cheap ones often taste like shit.

WAKAME: Edible green seaweed, sold either as thin strips (for seaweed salad) or in dried ribbons that need to be rehydrated in liquid. Once rehydrated, wakame has a texture that's somewhere between cooked greens and fruit peels. It tastes strongly of the ocean, with a subtle vegetal quality.

WASABI: Usually referred to as Japanese horse-radish, wasabi comes from the root of a river-dwelling plant. It has a nose-stinging bite that some people can't get enough of. Fresh wasabi is rare in the States (although there are now a few domestic growers) and extremely expensive. What you're most likely to find in a store is a paste in squeeze tubes or a powder that you mix with water. Either will be fine for the everyday purposes outlined in this book.

YUKARI: Rice seasoning made from dried red shiso. It's difficult to come by and not necessary for anything in this book, but if you can find it, it adds a really pleasant sourness and floral fragrance to rice dishes.

Thank-Yous

Did the world *need* us to write another cookbook? It's tough to say. But it fills us with hope and encouragement to have witnessed so many people working so hard to bring *The Gaijin Cookbook* to life. They've believed in this project from day one, and hopefully we've repaid their faith.

It begins with our agent, Kitty Cowles, who is perpetually thorough and protective and honest with us. 10 out of 10. Would recommend.

Kitty landed our book with the legendary Rux Martin and her team at Houghton Mifflin Harcourt—Sarah Kwak, Jamie Selzer, Melissa Lotfy, Eugenie Delaney, Jacinta Monniere, and Judith Sutton—who nurtured this project the whole way (and put up with a lot of bullshit too). Our designer, Walter Green, is one of the world's great talents and a living treasure. He made a beautiful book with art from Aubrie Pick, who is extremely good at taking pictures. Aubrie's team (Bessma Khalaf, Fanny Pan, Kristene Loayza, Glenn Jenkins, and Tallulah) set up shop with us for a week in Sebastopol, California, at the home of Chris's in-laws, Butch and Teri Witek. Butch and Teri were unbelievably gracious for opening their house to us (and allowing us to stress-eat all of their pistachios). We owe them big-time.

Shout-outs are also in order to some of our friends in Japan, who were endlessly patient and helpful as we wrote this book. Mizutani-san took our half-baked questions and turned them into a carefully thought-out itinerary. Thank you to Robbie Swinnerton and Nemo Glassman for showing us the coolest corners of Kyoto and Tokyo, and to chefs Kotaro-san, Kiharu-san, Yamauchi-san, Zaiyu-san, and Namae-san for feeding and educating us. And praise be to Eric and Ayako Jacobsen for watching our kids while we "researched" restaurants around town.

Some more people whom Chris would like to acknowledge:

As always, I'm nowhere and nothing without my family: Jami, Ruby, Mom, Dad, Louise, Michael, Andrew, Emma, Matthew, Huck.

I'm also grateful to all of my past and present colleagues at McSweeney's, Voice of Witness, *Lucky Peach*, MAD, and Majordomo Media for teaching me how to tell stories.

And, of course, Ivan. I'm a better dad and a better person for knowing you. I appreciate you calling just to shoot the breeze, even if I complain about it relentlessly. I really love this book we've made. My daughter is growing up eating food from *The Gaijin Cookbook*. Thank you.

And Ivan's personal thank-yous:

I would like to thank my wife, Mari, for believing in me no matter what. This book is for her and for my children, Isaac, Alex, and Ren, who give me purpose. Thank you to my family and friends, who never waver in their loyalty, and to my Ivan Ramen team: David Poran, Chad Combs, Dale Watkins, and Cat Brackett.

And to my partner, Chris, who has taught me so much about gathering experiences and knowledge from many places, and building something meaningful out of the pieces.

Index

Note: Page numbers in *italics* refer to photographs.